HYPERTUFA CONTAINERS

HYPERTUFA CONTAINERS

Creating and planting
an alpine trough garden

LORI CHIPS

Timber Press · Portland, Oregon

For
Joe and Mark
Adelle and Ervin

Frontispiece: Style can come from form. In this case, a nautilus shape planted with *Laurentia fluviatilis* and *Sempervivum arachnoideum*.

Photography credits appear on page 213.

Published in 2018 by Timber Press, Inc.
The Haseltine Building
133 S.W. Second Avenue, Suite 450
Portland, Oregon 97204-3527
timberpress.com

Printed in China
Cover design by Sarah Crumb
Text design by Patrick Barber

Library of Congress Cataloging-in-Publication Data

Names: Chips, Lori, author.
Title: Hypertufa containers: creating and planting an alpine trough garden /
    Lori Chips.
Description: Portland, Oregon : Timber Press, 2018. | Includes bibliographical
    references and index. |
Identifiers: LCCN 2018011957 (print) | LCCN 2018015767 (ebook) |
    ISBN 9781604698688 | ISBN 9781604697063 (pbk.)
Subjects: LCSH: Container gardening. | Container gardening—Equipment
    and supplies. | Alpine garden plants.
Classification: LCC SB418 (ebook) | LCC SB418 .C45 2018 (print) |
    DDC 635.9/86—dc23
LC record available at https://lccn.loc.gov/2018011957

A catalog record for this book is also available from the British Library.

Contents

PREFACE

I HAD MY FIRST AUTHENTIC encounter with troughs more than 20 years ago, while I was a student at the New York Botanical Garden's School of Professional Horticulture. Of course, I had seen images of troughs while wistfully looking through British garden books, sighing a little and making a mental note to learn more about them if the opportunity ever arose. Well, arise it did, while I was doing a rotation in the plant records department and was invited back to the Rock Garden greenhouse. Little did I know that during most of my horticultural career I would be devoting sizable chunks of every fall to designing and building these containers and finding my niche in the process.

I felt remarkably lucky to be invited, and accepted with alacrity. Jimmy Martucci, the senior rock gardener and an amazing gardener by any measure, created several troughs that day. He learned his skills and earned his wisdom the hard way—by doing. A large share of that doing was under the exacting eyes of the renowned T. H. Everett, under whose direction the New York Botanical Garden (NYBG) Rock Garden was born. I would later hear stories of the garden's creation, massive stones moved by resident horses who spent their leisure time stabled beneath the exquisite glass conservatory. During my tenure at NYBG, one could still see the delineation of the stalls. I have a deep respect for the experienced gardeners of that peer group. Many of those men were second generation Italians giving voice to the Latin names of plants in an engaging Bronx accent; their competence still, for me at least, has no equal.

Tabletop trough with a view.

7

There were a lot of things I didn't know that wintry afternoon as I stepped inside the Rock Garden potting shed. I was to spend many hours in the shelter of that shed, at that very potting bench. I would take fleets of cuttings, sow seed, and learn the fine points of show-potting alpines for the Rockefeller Center Flower Show. I would also bask in the camaraderie of many plant people, but especially of Jimmy, the man in charge of my trough-building education that day.

As he measured and mixed ingredients, he talked about his methods. We put on masks and gloves and he taught me about the construction of his wooden molds. Quickly, I warmed up to the task at hand and to the man himself. I learned that Jimmy was not only easy to work with, he was one of the most inventive gardeners I would ever know. His ingenuity was in evidence everywhere: from the work table that dropped down on hinges, to the storage areas where each spading fork and scuffle-hoe had its spot on the wall, to the ancient scythes threaded through the rafters overhead.

It was a warm space on a very cold day as I molded my first trough. When one works for any length of time in the ivory tower of a botanical garden, what becomes indelibly ingrained is the right way to do things, at least where plants are concerned. I am grateful for the depth of that ongoing lesson, dispensed with care, over time. It continues to inform what I do, especially in the creative process of trough making, and in the nurturing activity of growing plants.

That wonderful potting shed, its adjacent greenhouse, propagation unit, cold frames, and pit houses have long since been razed, victims of that terribly annihilating thing known as progress. And though for years Jimmy and I kept our connection, we lost touch some years after his retirement from NYBG. In my garden, I still have a trough he helped me make. A part of my spirit will always reside inside that cozy potting shed, busy on a winter afternoon, making troughs and many irreplaceable memories.

I've been making hypertufa troughs for two decades now, on a yearly basis, and I must admit that although my knowledge of the subject is thorough and extensive, it is also quirky. I have been lucky enough to be able to explore my creativity, to follow wherever inspiration or any bright idea would lead me. Not to give the impression that every trough shape is complicated. The list of classic, simple shapes is a worthy one: rectangle, cylinder, bowl, and oval among them. But sometimes in pushing the limits of a medium, technical problems with other simpler shapes are solved.

My good fortune has been due in part to working at a wonderful nursery (Oliver Nurseries) where finding and doing things that are cutting edge is a collective goal.

Once you fall under the spell of a trough, the hunt is on to find cool ways to fill them. The exploration of alpine plants is a vast enterprise in itself and it has pleasantly consumed a hefty slice of my gardening life. Because customers (for some reason) want plants that will live and perhaps even flourish, I have walked an interesting line with alpines. It is, roughly, a rule whereby I allow in about 30 percent difficult (or as they're often called, miffy) plants; the remaining 70 percent must have some staying power, some reliability. It is actually not a bad approach in any garden setting, permitting experimentation and risk taking with a manageable portion, while at the same time cultivating a more bulletproof population. The plant lists and recommendations I offer in this book are in that spirit, with the goal of a healthy chunk of success spiced up with some exotic, dangerous beauties to try if you have the fortitude to suffer heartache now and then.

I can't really remember a time when I wasn't writing. Of course, the form it took and the focus shifted over the years for many reasons. A person tends to write about what they spend time thinking about. So it has been with gardens, plants, and writing for me. I have been profoundly transformed by joining the North American Rock Garden Society (NARGS). The acknowledgments in this book are rife with NARGS members for good reason. I am blessed to call many of them friends, and each of them, without exception, has taught me something valuable.

In the newsletters of several NARGS chapters is where I began writing about plants. This was also where I discovered the work of the late Geoffrey Charlesworth, whose nametag and mine in the file box at the Berkshire chapter meetings were always together, because of the spelling of our last names. He was a droll expat Brit with an impeccable ear for good language. I avidly read both his books and they never go out of circulation for me. I return to them time and again and am always rewarded by rich, satisfying, ingenious writing and thinking. Reading these books is like visiting him in person. I can't add up all the times I wished for his thoughts as I completed pieces of this book. There is a story I like to relate about the first time I gave a talk. It was to knowledgeable NARGS members and I was understandably nervous. After it was over, Geoffrey came up and told me how much he had enjoyed it. I was pleased, but I said, "Well, I think I said the word 'um' a few too many times." "Nonsense," he said. "You said the word 'um' exactly the right number of times."

I hope that proves true about this work, too.

GETTING ENCHANTED

TROUGH GARDENING IS THE act of growing small plants, mostly alpines, in frost-resistant containers outdoors in all seasons. Originally these vessels were made of actual hewn stone. I will be focusing on man-made troughs designed to resemble genuine stone. That definition, however, doesn't even begin to express the appeal troughs have and the magic they bring once you set one down in your garden.

The charm of a planted trough coaxes the viewer to move closer, to pause in the pathway, to lean in. It is actually a piece of hardscape, after all, and has the ability to draw the eye in the same way an architectural detail, an ornate gate, or an armillary does. There is also an indescribable something about miniature things. Think of the devoted followers of toy trains, dollhouses, teacup poodles, and tiny ponies.

Hypertufa troughs are built either inside a mold or on the outside of a sand mold, and consist of a combination of portland cement, sieved peat moss, perlite, and fiber mesh. With a bit of preparation, construction can be accomplished in two half days. The reasons for building a trough are many. For one thing, they are not widely available for sale. Making your own also allows you to customize a trough for its setting or for a particular planting. Unlike many containers, they can withstand winter weather, and they make beautiful homes for miniature plants that might otherwise get lost or swamped in the open garden. A trough brings tiny plants up close to be viewed, while offering a protected environment. A trough is the jewel box for alpine treasures.

A jewel box of troughs.

Inviting closer examination.

SOME HISTORY

Trough gardening was first developed in Britain, probably for the Chelsea Flower Show. With the innovation of lightweight metal sinks, more cumbersome carved stone versions were being discarded and replaced. These included kitchen sinks as well as larger basins used for feeding and watering livestock. The stone ones could be had for a song. It was at this juncture that they began to be planted with miniature alpine plants. However, these distinguished old troughs were not always the best containers for alpines. Many were made of non-porous stone, making them little better than a plastic pot as far as finicky alpine roots were concerned. They were exceedingly heavy and many were also shallow. Some even lacked a drainage hole—not easy to fix in a mammoth chunk of stone.

A venerable carved stone trough.

Why Is It Called Hypertufa?

Hypertufa got its name from a natural rock called tufa. This is a type of limestone formed in streams or lacustrine environments in which there are a lot of suspended minerals. Tufa forms when these minerals precipitate out of the water and build up around organic materials such as moss and leaves. Eventually the organics decompose, and the final product is a rock with the exceptional porosity and structure of a sponge, though of course not soft and pliable. The roots of alpine plants love to grow right into the rock and the plants tend to thrive. Hypertufa is the alpine gardener's answer to the challenge of producing a man-made substance that borrows some of the growing attributes provided by genuine tufa. It is made from various aggregates bonded together with portland cement.

Beyond that, stone troughs are rare in America unless newly made. And whether antique or new, on this side of the pond or that, they are outrageously expensive. Enter the magic substance: hypertufa.

THE MANY REASONS TO TROUGH GARDEN

Hypertufa came about because of the desire for a substance that might help in the cultivation of alpine plants. The most important reason for growing in a hypertufa trough is that it improves your chances of success. Troughs are porous and frost resistant, and root systems of alpines love how cool the walls are. For plant geeks, a trough offers a shot at keeping that one crazy, rare, beloved treasure alive and possibly thriving.

Other people come to trough gardening because they have limited space to garden. Older gardeners with physical limitations can create a set-up requiring less bending and reaching. Then there's the matter of time. A trough takes literally one or two minutes to weed. Frequently, I hear of gardeners who have received a trough as a gift. It opens a new world for them. For the adventurous, a trough offers

Elevate troughs for convenience and beauty.

the opportunity to experiment, a chance to expand their plant vocabulary and flex their creativity.

This is not to say that troughs absolutely must be planted with alpine plants. There is no avenging trough angel who sweeps down upon unwitting acolytes, smiting with fury a trough stuffed with annuals or herbs or a voluminous shade perennial. With cold-hardy containers so hard to come by, though, it seems a waste of a trough to plant it with things that will perish at the first frost. I also think that much of the aesthetic magic goes unrealized when troughs are jammed with oversized leafy material.

When I give talks or demonstrations to new gardeners about the joys and demands of growing alpines in troughs, I usually focus on cultivation first and aesthetics second. Without sound horticultural practices, the plants won't thrive. Plants that

are thriving are beautiful—it is as simple as that. When I get to the aesthetic part, I try to invoke the artist in all of us. Designing a trough is an elegant and soulful discipline. But even in this decorative context, I provide some structure. Knowing the rules never hurt anyone. It gives you a place of strength on which to stand, before choosing a point of departure.

I struggle to put into words the particular appeal of a trough in the garden. It doesn't seem to matter if the trough in question is an ambitious tour-de-force landscape designed as a focal point, or an unassuming little bowl with just one plant. The effect it has resonates across the garden.

A friend and gifted designer I know highlighted this for me one day. He had resisted the lure of troughs for a long time. Finally, he bought a small, simple cylinder.

Plantings at the base of troughs integrate containers into the garden.

A miniature landscape with *Tsuga diversifolia* 'Loowit'.

In it he placed a tiny green butter pat of a plant, *Thymus serpyllum* 'Elfin'. This unassuming little container was placed among a rich collection of other potted plants on his patio. What happened with the addition surprised him. Without fail, every visitor, be they gardener or not, went straight to the trough, a forefinger pointed dramatically down at the thyme. "What," each one demanded, "is *that*?"

This was a bit of a eureka moment for me. Here is my best conclusion. A trough of whatever size is a theater. When the person in charge (that would be you) chooses to place a plant in this theater, everyone passing by wants to go to the show. They are intrigued: Why that plant, in that place, in that trough? It must mean something. And it almost always does.

THE MECHANICS
of TROUGH MAKING

T HE DEVIL IS IN the details, so they say, and nothing could be truer when it comes to trough making. My methods and recipes are not the only valid ones of course, but I will focus on the kind of observations of the process that were hard won for me and so may be useful to others. Hopefully these devils and details will prove to be valuable with subjects such as wall thickness, the gifts and treacheries of gravity, mix consistency, and how to fix an imperfect piece if it can possibly be done. If at times the information seems opinionated, well, it may be. I have spent a lot of years mixing a lot of hypertufa, making a lot of mistakes, and breaking my fair share of troughs to get to that opinion.

A major advantage of making your own trough is being able to choose among many variables: size, shape, depth, texture, and even color. A trough can be constructed precisely to suit the spot in which it will live. This is why it is worthwhile to don old clothes, drag a 94-pound bag of cement to your table or bench, and get to work.

Over the years, a whole bunch of words and phrases have been coined that apply to trough making. A few more have been borrowed or stolen from other disciplines when they seem to fit. It all amounts to a sort of troughing slang. I will try to define as I go, but I also include these terms in a glossary at the end of the book.

A range of creative trough possibilities.

19

The building of troughs seems to be shrouded in a sense of magic and mystery. I remember my first session, learning the techniques as a rite of passage, and that shroud added to the allure. It would be good to blow a clean wind of pragmatic know-how through the mist, though. Here goes.

BUILDING INSIDE A MOLD

The first trough-building method we'll tackle involves creating a trough by forming it *inside* a mold. In the next chapter, we'll discuss building troughs with sand molds, which entails forming the trough on the *outside* of the mold. Both are viable, popular ways to create beautiful planting vessels. Again, it's all a matter of what kind of trough style is desired.

Choosing the mold

As you consider molds, realize that because this trough will be built inside the mold, the final product will be just a bit smaller than what you are looking at. The mold must be either flexible or take-apart-able. If you use a hard wooden salad bowl, for example, you will lose the trough while trying to pry it loose and no doubt destroy the salad bowl as well. Flexible molds can be all sorts of plastic, vinyl, or rubber things, from an old shrub pot to a sweater box. Don't use anything as shallow as a kitty litter box. Depth is everything, because depth equals drainage. The plants are going to want root room; a shallow container is only useful for succulents, and that can be limiting.

Also, look carefully inside the mold. Are there suspicious ridges that will prevent the trough from sliding out? Is the bottom warped or grooved?

Take-apart molds can be constructed of wood (oil them before using) or Styrofoam (easier to build but not as long lasting.) Use screws instead of nails to secure Styrofoam. Duct tape around the outer box helps, too. Take-apart molds almost always have a second, smaller box that fits inside, leaving a gap around an inch and a half between the outer and inner boxes, to be filled with hypertufa. Generally, the mix is made wetter and of a more pourable consistency for these types of molds, to help the hypertufa fill out the mold with no gaps.

Most home hobbyists prefer working with flexible molds, using the patty-cake method, which will be explained. This is my favored method. It is flexible; almost anything can be created using this technique.

What You'll Need to Make a Hypertufa Trough

MATERIALS

pictured, left to right:

coarse perlite

peat moss, sieved

fiber mesh

portland cement, type I/II light

optional: cement colorant
    (*not pictured*)

TOOLS

5-gallon buckets

thin garbage bags of various sizes

thin mil plastic drop cloth, for lining the molds

thick mil plastic, to cover the table for all
    troughing projects, and to help with
    unmolding sand mold troughs

dust masks

waterproof gloves

wire brushes and other shaping tools

propane torch

builders sand (for sand molds)

wheelbarrow, deep (check for flat tires before
    you begin)

small cement hoe

shovel

1-quart plastic container

plastic containers (dishpans, plastic bins) to fill
    with hypertufa and carry to the table

hose with shutoff, watering wand

small watering can

Finally, if you have your heart set on creating an oil jar, you are flat out of luck. There is no mold that will work for this. The pesky laws of physics prevent us from unmolding a piece out of, or off of, any shape with a narrow neck. (But a way to cheat this is described in the next chapter.)

THE SET-UP

Always insist on a set-up day if you do not want to be mixing your first batch of hypertufa at three or four in the afternoon. Getting prepared always takes longer than anticipated. Having a list and purchasing supplies is only the beginning; you also must decide where it all will happen. Figuring out an appropriate place to make your troughs is not as easy as you might think. If the weather is nice, you can, of course, plan to do it outside, but what if it rains? This project takes (at least a portion of) two days to complete, so build that into the plan.

This would be a good time to talk about the concept of "mess." I thought I knew what a mess was before I made troughs. I quickly realized how vast the gradations of a true mess are, and that I had previously been a relative lightweight in this realm. This project can produce the most enormous, insidious, under-your-skin mess imaginable—one that has the propensity to damage things and you. Tables and floors are obvious; driveways, lawns, and lungs less so but still vulnerable. Not to mention everything you wear. Once you have worn an item of clothing to trough in, troughing will be its purpose from then on. Clothes don't come back from this. Neither does footwear. It is also hard on fingernails and hair, but that is from the viewpoint of someone whose troughing season goes on for five to seven weeks.

Therefore, select your site with care and realize that cement will drop, and weather can change. Under cover of some kind is best. I strenuously advise setting up a table on which to do the work; your back will be eternally grateful. Check that it is a comfortable height for you. Also make sure it is rock solid, it will have to bear some serious weight.

Some whys and wherefores of what you'll need

COLORANTS I'm all for playing with interesting aspects of trough making. However, I've seen some pretty bad errors in judgment when it comes to tinting. A batch of hypertufa is a lot of work and committing to a color for the whole thing is a big investment. The colors are not subtle, either. With both wet colorant and dry powder, one never knows how much to add, because the mix is wet while you work with it. The shade will be entirely different once the trough has dried—lighter, brighter, often garish. If colorant is blended completely into the mix, it comes out uniform. That said, I sometimes have fun adding charcoal gray to sand mold pieces, or a blend of a couple of colors. I add a splotch or two with heavy colorant, then graduate the color by adding a smaller amount moving away from the initial patch. I work the rims of some pieces, darker on one side usually. My approach is similar to that of a potter applying glaze before firing, except you can't just apply this to the surface. If you do, you may wire brush all the color off in the finishing process.

A subtle use of colorant on one side. Clockwise from top: *Penstemon procerus* var. *tolmiei* 'Bethel Ridge', *Calluna vulgaris* 'Firefly', *Sempervivum* 'Gold Nugget', *Penstemon davidsonii* 'Microphyllus', *Sempervivum* 'Lilac Time', *Sedum album* 'Coral Carpet', and *Orostachys iwarenge*.

I only add colorant to a small dishpan of wet hypertufa instead of a whole wheelbarrow, and then just to one side of the mass as I work with it, so that I have a plain side and a dyed side in the dishpan itself.

FIBER MESH This is a poly fiber and not fiberglass. It is available at masonry supply stores and was invented to be mixed into cement for paving purposes. It prevents tiny microcracks as they start. If a crack hits a fiber, it stops. That's the theory, anyway. It strengthens the trough and eliminates the need for a chicken wire armature, the method that was used in the bad old days. Those fiendish things were hard to form, ripped into even well-gloved hands, were difficult to cover with hypertufa, and often showed through on the finished trough. When buying fiber mesh, avoid a substandard product sometimes called "reinforcing fiber." It clumps into fuzz balls and will make your carving and finishing sessions miserable.

Some trough makers believe that using a bonding agent in the mix strengthens the trough. I have never found it to make an appreciable difference. It's an extra step and extra expense. This material mostly seems to be recommended for fusing something to existing hardened cement, including patching and repairing. I don't recommend it for hypertufa trough mixtures.

PEAT MOSS It *must* be sieved through a medium mesh such as quarter-inch hardware cloth. This is easier if the mesh is stapled to a frame. Sieving screens out big chunks of peat and pieces of wood. If you skip this step, you will live to regret it. Those obnoxious pieces will always end up on the front rim of your best trough.

PLASTIC CONTAINERS These are one of those practical things you wish you had rounded up before you started, so do it first. Even if you place the wheelbarrow right next to your table, you will be leaning over it repeatedly, scooping up hypertufa. Save your back. This also allows you to customize the wetness of the medium to your liking, by dribbling in a small amount of water.

PORTLAND CEMENT This is the only kind of cement to use. It is a type of cement, not a brand name or place of origin. Type I/II is the one I use. The color can be a bit variable; whiter, grayer, or browner are possibilities. Troughs generally take on a more natural coloration after weathering outdoors for a few seasons. It is foolhardy to even think of trying the fast-drying sorts like Quikrete. You will spend enough time and effort on this to not want it to fail because of rash ingredient choices. Cement only comes in 94-pound bags. I have always thought that the company who decides to market cement in reasonably sized bags would gain a fair patronage among those, myself included, who would rather shoulder a less spine-crushing weight.

Screen out bigger pieces of peat moss.

SAND You will need to decide whether or not to use sand in your mixture. I personally don't like it; it changes the texture and makes the finished product much heavier. However, if you plan to build troughs on sand molds, you will have to get sand anyway. For building molds, you will need more than you think. Since these molds are free form and whatever size you decide, predicting an exact amount is impossible. Half a yard of builders sand will work out well if several of you are building sand molds and you plan to make a number of batches. If you are by yourself and not ambitious about size, start with four or five 50-pound bags.

SHAPING TOOLS These can be anything that works; be inventive. During trough season, my mental radar gets tuned to this. Walking through a hardware store (or any store for that matter) I am always thinking, "Will that object be a good scraper? Would that bin be an interesting mold?" Besides wire brushes, good tools to have on hand include paint scrapers (several sizes, both rigid and flexible), an old knife or two, a screwdriver, and cement trowels (both the pie-server shape and rectangular). But best of all, try to lay your hands on some clay-sculpting tools. Many clay tools are too flimsy to work cement, so always go for the strongest. Tools that can be resharpened are important, too. The absolute best in the business are Dolan Tools. They disappeared from the market for several years and my heart was broken. I babied the few I had. Dolan is now back, but you need to make wise choices because they are not cheap. The ones to get are the heavy duty loops known as Dolan faceting tools. They are well made and well tempered. And no, I don't own stock in the company. It's just that these implements hold up to the job, and the blades don't separate from the handles. They help you create the shape or the finished look you want. In fact, with a container full of tools, when I have classes, everybody goes for the Dolans first.

MAKING THE HYPERTUFA

Before getting started, protect yourself. Glove up and wear a dust mask! If you are using the thin latex medical gloves, wear two pairs because they tear easily, and cement is caustic. First, slather a generous glob of moisturizer onto your hands. Products that include cocoa butter, vitamin E, and shea butter will both help the gloves slide on and benefit your hands. No matter how careful you plan to be, you are going to get hypertufa on your skin, even under your nails. Also, please choose a good dust mask, even a respirator. Fine particles from peat, perlite, and cement are not good for your lungs. If working inside, I always move the wheelbarrow outside to do the mixing, preserving a less dusty environment inside. Before opening a bag of cement, make sure you have all the ingredients you will need. Spread the heavy mil plastic over the work surfaces, making sure the plastic doesn't trail on the floor, where it could trip you up. Trim to fit if need be, allowing some overhang.

This is a good juncture for a word about timing your mixes. You want to be done by dark. Therefore, I advise first-time trough makers to plan the mix for morning or early afternoon, to leave yourself plenty of time. Remember, the mix has to be used up, troughs sealed in plastic, and tools cleaned before walking away for the day. I've had to wash out too many wheelbarrows with ice-cold hose water in the dark to not warn you to plan ahead.

Hypertufa Mix Recipe

(buckets referenced are 5-gallon)

Separate the fiber mesh while adding it to a hand-mixed batch.

> **1½ buckets of coarse perlite**
> **¾ bucket of sieved peat moss**
> **1 full bucket portland cement, type I/II light**
> **1 good-sized handful of fiber mesh**

In very broad terms, depending on mold size, depth, wall thickness, and other variables, this amount of mixture will make roughly four small to medium-size troughs. For two smaller or one large trough, halve the recipe.

1. PLACE THE INGREDIENTS IN THE WHEELBARROW. Follow the order listed, because perlite has a tendency to float up and both the cement and peat tend to travel down.

2. SCATTER THE FIBER MESH ACROSS THE TOP. Separate it somewhat as you scatter.

3. MIX THE DRY INGREDIENTS THOROUGHLY. Make sure there are no pockets of perlite or peat anywhere.

Do You Need a Mechanical Mixer?

If you happen to have easy access to a cement mixer, then by all means use it. It is important to know, however, that all cement mixers are not created equal. There is a difference between a mortar mixer and a cement mixer. A cement mixer is the barrel type, where the barrel itself rotates and there are stationary blades inside to do the work. A mortar mixer has rotating blades inside that do the mixing, often with rubber strips that help scrape the material off the sides. The main body of the machine does not move, except to tilt the finished mixture out. This mortar-mixer style is the kind you want. You do *not* want the fixed blades inside the barrel; fiber mesh forms the worst kind of hairballs with this mixer. My experience with the stationary blade configuration has been a total disaster. In one case, we had to remove half the material to the wheelbarrow and mix that by hand with a hoe and shovel. The other half inside the machine needed so much water that it was sopping wet. We walked away in disgust to take a good long lunch. Even after that, it was still too wet and filled with dense fiber mesh hairballs.

With mobile paddles inside the drum, the paddles do the mixing *and* help disgorge the mass into the wheelbarrow once mixing is done. These are heavy machines, not for the infirm or the faint of heart. *Never* disable or remove the safety cage, or any other safeguard on the machine. The downside, even with a good mixer, is the strength needed to move the machine, pour the dry cement in, and empty the contents. There are a lot of safety rules you must follow; a mixer is definitely an accident waiting to happen for the uninitiated. It doesn't really save time over manual mixing. And you must wash out and truly clean the machine after every use. Even if you intend to make another batch that afternoon, it can't be left sloppy. On the plus side: it can save your back and you can mix up double batches at a time.

4. ADD WATER SLOWLY. Add the water in stages and mix between additions, until the mixture reaches the consistency of rather thick oatmeal. If the mix is too dry, the chemical process that bonds the mixture will be impeded. I have seen my fair share of failed troughs that were too crumbly even after curing because there was too *little* water mixed in to start off the chemical process. If the mix is too wet, wait 15 or 20 minutes. The consistency may correct itself as the dry peat absorbs water. Or, you can add dry ingredients proportionately. I keep a plastic one-quart container handy for measuring or adding small amounts of ingredients. You can also use it to measure and mix up a tiny batch in a pan on those occasions when you run out and need just a little bit more to complete a trough.

Follow these steps and hopefully the Goddess of Hypertufa Consistency will bless you with perfect mixes. Just remember, She never blesses you 100 percent of the time.

For more on mix consistency, see the section titled Gravity, Consistency, and Carving Excess on page 30.

The right consistency is important.

Forming the Trough

There is something intrinsically satisfying and primeval about sinking your hands into this medium and creating a vessel. Tribes have been working like this for centuries to make everything from sacred cups to plates in which they smashed corn. Trough making is your chance to join the tribe.

You have your chosen mold in hand and it has passed all scrutiny. The hypertufa is mixed; you are ready to go.

1. WET DOWN THE INSIDE OF YOUR MOLD COMPLETELY. It is handy to keep a watering wand ready to use, as well as at least one small watering can.

2. LINE THE MOLD WITH THE THIN MIL PLASTIC DROP CLOTH. The thin mil adheres best to the wet mold. Try to minimize folds and creases by *intentionally* pleating and making flat tucks in the sheet. This way it is easier to avoid folds occurring unpredictably and hurting the integrity of the piece. By the way, kitchen plastic wrap is never wide enough, sticks to itself, and is a pain to work with. Go with drop cloth.

3. MAKE CERTAIN THERE ARE A FEW INCHES OF OVERHANG ON ALL SIDES, THEN CUT TO FIT.

4. PAT THE HYPERTUFA INSIDE THE MOLD. A handful at a time, begin to form the bottom of the trough by patting the hypertufa in

Minimize folds.

Bring a portion of mix to your work table.

After installing the bottom, begin building the walls.

place. This is called the patty-cake method. The exact techniques of the patty-cake method and the consistency of the mix is open slightly to preference, but you don't want a pourable mixture or the mold would need an insert to retain the walls. When you patty-cake the piece together, the medium must have more body and be able to stand up on its own. Within reason, the thickness of the walls is a matter of choice. Make them thinner than three-quarters of an inch and the piece may be too fragile. Make them thicker than two inches (depending on the overall size of the mold) and the aesthetics may not be pleasing. I can tell you unequivocally that elegant is much better than a clunky porridge bowl that looks like it came from the Black Forest in the Middle Ages.

A terrific back saver is having those small empty containers (without holes) for scooping up mix and carrying it to your workspace. Anything waterproof and lightweight works. This offers the added benefit of allowing each artisan to customize the moisture in the mix. Just as the needs of each piece vary, so do the preferences of each trough maker.

5. BEGIN BUILDING UP THE SIDES OF THE TROUGH. I like to work in courses, similar to building a stone or brick wall. Err on the side of a slightly dryer mix in the bottom course or two, as a wetter mix will travel downward. Take the time to press the mix into the corners to prevent gaps. This is a little like making a coil pot, a structure that potters know well. You are using each handful of material to make overlapping joins to form courses up the wall of your mold. You can use the sides of the mold to press against as long as you are also pressing the handfuls to form a bond with the preceding course. Gently and carefully firm each new handful onto the last so that no weak spots develop. Bring the walls up to the desired height. The deeper you make the trough, the more plant choices you will have.

6. POKE DRAINAGE HOLES. Once finished, use a screwdriver or your finger to poke an adequate number of drainage holes in the bottom, being careful not to weaken the structure with too many, or with holes too close together. Make one hole three-quarters of an inch to one and a half inches for a trough twelve inches square or less; add more holes for larger or longer troughs. Cover the trough and the mold well with plastic and allow it to set up for the night.

7. FINISH UP. At the end of the day, the mix must be used up or thrown away (which is painful, after all your careful work of mixing!). It will not hold until the next day, and could ruin whatever you try to hold it in (the wheelbarrow, for instance). Instead, use up leftover mix by making a tiny trough to hold succulents that don't mind a shallow pot. All tools need to be cleaned, and the wheelbarrow must be washed out.

Firm each handful so it bonds with the preceding one.

GRAVITY, CONSISTENCY, AND CARVING EXCESS

Gravity, for the trough maker, can be a nemesis. For that reason, *do not overwork the mixture*. Too much kneading and patting changes the structure and wetness of the mix, causing walls to slump. Except for outright breakage, nothing frightens a trough neophyte more than this phenomenon, and believe me, you will know it when you see it. (Conversely, too little kneading and patting can leave the joins poorly bonded and thus weak. Strive for a middle ground.) If the surface of the hypertufa is beginning to get shiny, you may be overworking it. In masonry terms, this is the "butter" stage. While acceptable in sidewalk paving, it creates problems in troughs. If the dreaded slumping has started, the walls will be thick and glossy, out of shape, and sliding toward the bottom. You may see a lot of excess water in the bottom. The bottom itself may have become a good deal thicker, too. One way to circumvent this state is to work on two troughs at the same time. Simply switch back and forth from one trough to the other between each course or two, thereby allowing the medium to set up a little in between.

When all else fails and slumping is already underway, go have some tea.

Enclose the trough and mold in plastic overnight.

Holding a Batch

There comes a moment in every trough maker's life when you still have another trough or two in you, the batch is not used up, but you need to take an intermission. Perhaps you have tackled a complex sand mold. It's almost two o'clock and no lunch yet—you could really use a break. This is when you need to know how to "hold" a batch.

Although hypertufa must be used up in a reasonably timely fashion, it does not go bad or set up as rapidly as you might imagine. The ambient temperature has a lot to do with how speedily it sets up; warmer equals faster.

To hold it, generously sprinkle the barrowful with a little extra water, perhaps chopping it into the mix a bit with a shovel. Press a big garbage bag or other plastic covering over the top, making direct contact with the mix, and roll the wheelbarrow into a shaded spot. Then feel free to leave. Your window of time to use up the mix can be anywhere from two to four hours. The telltale sign that time is running out is when the mix starts heating up to the touch. That means the chemical process that drives the curing of the cement is underway, and it behooves you to get cracking. At moments like this, pull out your biggest mold or do a quick, down-and-dirty sand kidney trough in a large size to use up the senescent mix.

Carving when wet

Upon your return from tea, tentatively touch the trough with your finger (gloved up again, of course). It may seem a good deal firmer. However, chances are that this intermission has brought the hypertufa to what, in clay pottery terms, is called the "leather" stage. If you attempt to push the stuff into some kind of shape, it is likely to crack or tear. Instead I propose the following.

Using a knife or a sharp paint scraper (please, do not use your glorious loop tools for this), begin to slice away some of the extra thickness from inside the trough. This takes a certain touch, so proceed gently. Try for a consistent wall thickness, if you can.

Carve until you are pleased with your work, remembering that the finishing process tomorrow will correct many imperfections. Lastly, cover your mold well or insert it into a plastic bag to set up for the night. Never allow it to freeze at this point.

Unmolding the Trough

The next day, remove the bag and test for firmness. How soon is too soon to unmold? If it was a warm night, it may be getting close to too late. Get busy early in the morning if this is the case, as it could be a tough scrape-down. In general, any amount of time from 12 to 36 hours will set the hypertufa enough to work with it. I know that is a little like saying, "Boil the vegetables from 12 to 48 minutes." It is barely useful and can result in food that is either raw or mush. But with the setting up of hypertufa, there are just too many variables to give hard and fast rules. The size of the trough is important. It may seem counterintuitive, but larger troughs harden up much faster; they have more mass that heats up in the curing process. Overnight temperature is another factor, as is humidity, thickness of the walls, what time of day it was completed, how quickly it was covered, whether or not it was in the sun, how wet the mix was to start with, and so on. So you must test.

Test for hardness, then finish the inside first.

1. SCRAPE THE SURFACE GENTLY. Use a wire brush, a paint scraper, or a clay loop if you have one. Scrape these lightly against the surface. Do not be fooled by shininess. Some of the hardest, most overset pieces I have ever worked on have looked as glossy as very wet ones.

If the brush grabs and pulls clumps out of the surface, it is too soft. If you run the loop over the surface and it rolls up whole pieces of perlite, it is too soft. What you want is for the loop to *slice through* the pieces of perlite, cutting them in half instead of uprooting and rolling them out. That will mean the hypertufa has hardened enough to hold those particles in place, an excellent indicator that it is time for brushing, shaping, and finishing.

Place your fingers over the trough edge and mold rim while inverting.

2. IF THE MATERIAL HAS HARDENED ENOUGH, PROCEED TO TEXTURING. At this point, the trough is still inside a mold. Finish all interior surfaces to your liking, except the rim; one has more control gauging the look of that once it is unmolded. Clear

Lift the mold off.

Carefully peel back the plastic.

the drainage hole(s) with a screwdriver or nail. If you used a plastic shrub pot for a mold, be sure to trim off the excess hypertufa bulging out of the pot's drainage holes on the outside. If you neglect this, the trough will refuse to slide out of the mold.

3. USING TWO HANDS, INVERT THE TROUGH ONTO A FLAT WORK SURFACE. At this stage, the trough may still be quite fragile. Lift off the mold and gently peel off the plastic. If plastic has become embedded anywhere in a crease, cut it off with scissors, don't pull it out. That could damage the trough by popping out a large divot. The burning-off step later will eliminate any visible plastic. It is hard to remember sometimes, but never grab, move, or push your trough with one hand. It is still soft enough to break off in your hand. Always use two hands as a precaution and even then, do not hold it by the rim. The sad truth is, if you end up making a lot of troughs, it won't be "if" you break one, but "when." Help the odds as best you can.

A word of caution. Most troughs that break do so on the reflip, when the trough is being turned back to right-side up. Always use two hands to lift the trough; pretend it is an eggshell that might crack and don't put undue pressure on the walls. If the medium seems soft and you have concerns about breakage, you can leave the trough, still in its mold but uncovered, exposed to air for an hour or even longer. If it is unmolded but still seems vulnerable to breakage, leave it alone, upside down, in the position it was in when you slid the mold off. By all means, brush down or scrape the exposed surfaces. Come back to it before the end of the day, certainly before it has really begun to dry out, reflip it, and finish texturing the rim.

FINISHING

You have arrived at the fun part! It is time to use brushes, clay tools, scrapers, and anything else you have handy to shape, sculpt, correct imperfections, and texture your trough. Brushing will raise the fiber mesh on the surfaces, making them look fuzzy. This will be burned off later.

Many imperfections and mishaps can be mitigated or finessed if you are clever and think outside the box. Outright breakage cannot be repaired. It's best to accept the small tragedies, learn from them and then go on creating. If an edge is broken, carve it down into a lower edge on that side and plan to plant a cascading plant there. Or, simply make the height of the walls shorter overall. A shallower trough is better than no trough at all. (And next time you will remember not to pull it toward you by the rim with one hand.)

This might be a good time to inject my opinionated views on the theme of elegance, because a trough either has it, or it doesn't. What I try to aim for is a "felt balance." For example, the wall thickness and height do not have to be the identical measurement at every point (almost impossible to achieve). But the walls ought to look and feel evenly thick and tall. Ultimately, these are handcrafted objects, not machine-made ones. We wouldn't want them to look mass produced. But almost without exception, it is the edge wherein lives this elusive elegance that I strive for. For troughs, elegance generally means a thinner wall and an edge that is flat and sharp or beveled. I have even done a quick (though not even close to scientific) poll. I lined up a number of troughs all created within the same mold, but all finished by different people. They had different edges, thicknesses, and looks. I asked which of them would sell first. Invariably, the ones with relatively thin walls and clean edges got nominated. By everyone. No one wants something too clunky or thick.

In this quest for elegance, sometimes a batch of troughs has gone past the easy-to-carve stage, for whatever reason. There is still hope. Except for the hardest, driest troughs, the rim can be fixed by cheating the edge. You can chisel, using a sharp, rigid paint scraper and a mallet, but you do not need to do the whole wall. When the material is this tough to work on, every inch is hard won. If just the top edge itself has been narrowed, the illusion is that the entire wall is thinner. Once planted up, there is no telling the difference.

Use a clay tool to texture the outside.

Bag and seal the trough for its curing period.

Burn off the fuzzy fiber mesh.

Finished but not yet weathered.

Curing

The curing of hypertufa is not the same as drying. Curing is a chemical process and moisture must be present for it to work. You can even feel the heat build up in the medium when this is underway. Once you have finished the trough, clear away any debris from inside and underneath (this debris has a penchant for re-adhering to the finished surface and can be hard to remove later). Open a properly sized plastic bag and, using two hands, slip it inside. Seal the bag by tying it. The trough should stay sealed for at least four weeks; eight to twelve is better. The longer you leave it enclosed to cure, the stronger the trough will be. Once again, it must not be allowed to freeze at this point.

Burning Off

After the long curing period, remove the trough from the bag. Allow it to dry for several days before firing up the propane torch to burn off all the fiber mesh and any leftover plastic caught in a seam. Do not hold the flame on any one spot for too long; this can cause tiny pockets of moisture to boil and a crack to form, or even a fragment to fly out. *Do not ever wear plastic, rubber, vinyl, or latex gloves for this procedure.* If the worst should happen, a skin burn is made many, many times more serious if these materials melt into it. Observe all safety precautions rigorously—protect your eyes, read the labeling on the torch before getting started, stay alert, and use common sense. It should go without saying that the burning off needs to be performed in a space devoid of easily ignited materials. No trough, no matter how handsome, is worth an injury.

Weathering

The cement in hypertufa contains free lime, which is harmful to plants. This must be leached out. If you make troughs in the fall they can, after curing, be left outside to allow precipitation to accomplish this. Eight

A new collection waiting for moss spores.

weeks is a minimum. When rainfall is inadequate, it helps to periodically hose them down.

There are many preparations to encourage the growth of algae and mosses, if this is the look you want. Paint on some buttermilk, diluted yogurt, beer, or the water in which rice, corn, or potatoes have been cooked. I personally found out how well this works the year we built our fieldstone patio. After it was finished, we had many occasions to entertain outdoors. As time went on, I noticed that one half of the patio had grown a thick, lush velvet of moss between the stones. The exposure was the same on both sides of the patio. I wondered what caused the moss on only one side. Then one day it dawned on me. We always boiled a big pot of corn on the cob for company in the summer. At the end of the evening, I poured the corn water out on that side of the patio. The sugars and starches in the cooking water did the trick. Another time-honored method to promote mosses is simply rubbing the surface with the cut side of a potato. Manure tea and stagnant pond water have also been effective. For any of these methods to succeed, though, moss spores must be present in the area.

THE ART *of* TROUGH MAKING: SAND MOLDS

I MUST ADMIT TO A deep affinity for the sand mold method of creating troughs, in which troughs are formed on the *outside* of the mold. Over the years I have pushed the boundaries of this technique pretty hard, and it has been fun, inspiring, and challenging all at the same time. Hypertufa is a very plastic medium; the permutations are vast. Its only limiting characteristic is the issue of supporting the shape while it is wet. Of course, the next day, when that shape is no longer malleable, there also must be an easy way to remove the support—and in this regard, sand is matchless as a mold. It can be crumbled and brushed away. There is an art to the actual molding process, and there is also an art to building the sand mold. Instead of locating a shape you like and filling it, this is a concept process: the shape of your next trough begins in your imagination. Potters, ceramicists, and glass workers often push these frontiers. Trough builders rarely do.

Working with a sand mold can free the artist in all of us. Many shapes can be created in no other way. I recommend getting some experience under your belt creating troughs inside traditional molds, however, before attempting this more complex technique. To get the feeling of sand as a mold, it is also good to begin with one of the simpler shapes.

Some simple troughs built on sand forms.

Making a Sand Mold

1. CLEAR YOUR WORK TABLE AND MAKE VERY SURE IT IS A COMFORT-ABLE HEIGHT. I know I stressed this in the previous chapter on regular molds, but they were portable; a mold with the trough inside it can be moved. When you embark on a sand mold, you are stuck where you are for the duration. Your table must be able to take the weight of the hypertufa plus the damp sand.

2. COVER THE TABLE WITH HEAVY MIL PLASTIC.

3. PILE CLEAN BUILDERS SAND ON THE SURFACE. Make a heap just a little smaller than you want your finished trough to turn out. Leave enough room all around the heap to form the trough on the tabletop. (I have seen people build a gorgeous sand mold only to realize there was just not enough space around it on the table to apply the mix.) Unlike working inside a mold where the trough ends up a bit smaller than the mold, this trough will be substantially bigger than the sand mold you create. Bigger by the combined widths of the walls, and taller because of the bottom you add on top. With sand molds, you must get used to a process of thinking upside down and inside out.

Shapes and textures made on sand.

The sand mold you build equals the root space for your plants in the finished trough. To create depth, which in this case equals how high you build the sand mold, the sand itself must be adequately moistened. If you remember building sandcastles at the beach with upturned buckets, you know the right consistency and dampness. The sand should not be so dry that it will not hold a shape, but neither should it be sloppy wet. You should be able to pack it into place easily.

It is a good idea to invent your shape(s) in sand before mixing the hypertufa. If this is your first experience with this type of mold, choose simpler forms that don't depend on hard-edged geometry. Pack sand firmly into place and dampen when needed. Keep a spray bottle of water nearby, but don't overdo the wetness. Cement trowels are a great help with shaping, as is a small, perfectly flat board to level what will be the bottom. When you feel satisfied, step back and imagine it turned right-side up. You will likely notice something you want to correct. The bottom is not quite flat, the walls should be steeper, an oval may be too round. If you are aiming for symmetry, check that angles and curves mirror each other. Use a critical eye.

4. HELP RIM TEXTURE BY FLOURING. Before applying hypertufa to the sand mold, I use a trick to produce a pleasing texture on the trough's rim. It is a well-known baker's trick called flouring, which means lightly sprinkling a surface with flour before working with dough on the surface. In this case, scoop up some bone-dry sand and lightly flour the surface of the plastic table cover all around the base of the mold. When hypertufa mixtures are left to set up pressed against a smooth surface like plastic, they come out shiny. If for some reason you must delay unmolding the piece, a sand-floured rim will be textured already, instead of glossy and difficult to work. Use a light hand when sprinkling the dry sand; the benefit of the nice flat table is that it produces a nice flat rim. Flouring too much will make the rim uneven and lumpy.

Create a kidney shape in sand.

Be certain the trough bottom is flat.

Upon flouring, you will immediately notice any water seeping out into the dry sand, revealing that your mold may be too wet. A little seepage is okay, but sopping wet is not. Allowing time for the mold to dry is the only remedy for a too-wet sand mold. If you doggedly proceed, the wetness at the rim will mix with the hypertufa edge and degrade it. You will end up with thin spots, or even divots in the edge, impossible to correct. Better to come back to this one later or even the next day.

Lightly flour with dry sand the surface where the rim will be.

Applying the Hypertufa

Most of the same procedures apply that would be used to form a trough inside a mold. I have never understood why some people recommend covering a sand mold with plastic before applying hypertufa. When the mixture sets against a slick surface, it ends up smooth and glassy. This is not good for the health of the plant roots (not porous), nor for the appearance of the finished product. A good deal more slumping occurs when the mix has only a slick surface to which it can cling. Eliminate the plastic and two things happen. You don't have to worry about roughing up the inside of the trough; the sand textures it for you. And because you need not worry about how hard a brush-down it will be (on the inside), you can leave the mold undisturbed in its place for a lot longer to set up, thus lessening the threat of breakage.

1. CONSTRUCT THE FIRST COURSE, THE RIM. It is always worthwhile to slow down and pay extra attention here, because the rim is very visible on the finished trough. Take the time to ensure a consistent rim width.

Spend extra attention on the rim, the most visible part of the finished trough.

2. WORK WITH A HANDFUL OF HYPERTUFA AT A TIME. Press down firmly against the table but without undue pressure against the sand mold. You obviously cannot press as hard against the sand as you could against a plastic or wooden mold. Instead, as you continue building courses, you are massaging the handfuls down against the previous course. As always, try to find the right touch.

3. MAKE SURE THE OVERLAPPING JOINS ARE WELL INTE-GRATED. They should become invisible as you bond them, otherwise you may be opening the door for cracks, even possible breakage. Judging the thickness and uniformity of the walls is a little trickier in this case; a piece of wire, a pencil or a long nail can be inserted right into the wall to measure this (be sure to close up any resulting holes).

4. PACK EXTRA SAND AGAINST THE OUTSIDE OF THE TROUGH. This step is optional, but many find it helpful in supporting the trough walls during construction, especially with some shapes. Do not scatter sand between courses of hypertufa, however, which will weaken the joins. Sand against the outside is very helpful if a wall starts to fall away from the mold or starts to slump. Slumping manifests differently with a sand mold than inside a plastic mold. With a sand mold, hypertufa will either begin to pull away from the mold, usually when the walls are more vertical, or it will become ever thicker at the rim, which is now the lowest point. Slumping will cause you to make very little progress in raising the walls. Shoring up with sand outside is a good remedy; just make sure the rim is not impossibly thick already. Remember that the bigger the piece and the more vertical the walls, the more likely you will hit that wobble point. The only real downside of the sand brace outside is that where you shore it up, you cease to have a visual reference to judge shape and symmetry. I always thought I'd have no trouble retaining shape memory as I worked. With simple forms, it is relatively easy. But the bigger and more complex the shape, the harder it gets. Troughs built on a sand mold usually have some kind of small surprise for you upon unmolding anyway; they are a little unpredictable. Elaborate ones have bigger surprises. I enjoy this aspect and use it as a springboard for something new and different. It's where some of the art comes into play.

5. BUILD YOUR LAST WALL COURSE ABOVE THE LEVEL OF THE SAND MOLD. While gravity makes for too-thick bottoms in upright plastic molds, here, upside down, the medium wants to

Take care that each course is bonded to the last.

Create a "well" for a flat bottom.

Wet some mix to create a slurry.

A nice flat bottom.

flow downward toward the rim and away from the bottom. By raising your wall about one and a half inches higher than the sand, you can help avoid a too-thin bottom.

6. ENSURE A FLAT BOTTOM. This step eliminates a chronic problem with sand molds: rounded bottoms, which cause the trough to not sit right. Inexperienced trough makers tend to simply patty-cake the bottoms on. The best method is to take a pan of the hypertufa mix and make it substantially wetter. This mixture is called a slurry and should be almost pourable.

7. DUMP THE SLURRY ON TOP (THE EVENTUAL BOTTOM) OF THE TROUGH. Smooth into place, working the mixture to eliminate any pockets or air holes. This is one case where overworking is a good thing. The aforementioned inch and a half or so of extra wall will contain it. The wet mix should be like a thin mud and will find its own level with just a little help from you. If the final course came up sufficiently high, you should have a perfect bottom. If it is wet enough, it will certainly be flat. When flipped over it will sit level.

8. MAKE DRAINAGE HOLES IN THE BOTTOM.

9. COVER WITH PLASTIC. Weight the edges with sand.

10. POLICE THE TABLETOP. Check around before leaving things for the night. If you plan to reuse the sand for new trough molds, discard clumps and clods of half-hardened cement. If this gets mixed back into the sand, the sand will become increasingly hard to work with. (For the same reason, when shaping the trough the next day, make sure there is a drop cloth covering any exposed heaps of sand on the table.) If possible, the trough can be moved to an empty space for finishing, keeping the carved-off detritus from being mixed with the sand.

A kidney-shaped mold before (right) and after (left) hypertufa application. Don't forget the drainage holes!

Texturing the Surface

Sand does not provide support for the trough the same way a plastic or wooden mold does. However, it is still very important to wire brush, scrape, or otherwise finish the outside of the trough the day after molding it. So, as you apply texture, do not use undue pressure against the surfaces.

Commonly, texturing a trough is all about giving it a pleasing and uniform finish. This means different things to different artisans, and it can vary from trough to trough. For one shape, the look of a clean, flat veneer is exactly right. On a rounded form, consistent wire brush strokes circling the piece can feel natural and beautiful.

There are also times when it is not simply a matter of texture. Perhaps the surface is already pretty hard. In cases like this,

Create the texture you want.

Deep texturing in a trough has drama all its own.

I sometimes go for a sculpted look. It can feel like a real workout, but chiseling a surface to resemble actual hewn stone is a great effect. Deeply striating a container with a sharp tool adds a whole new level of sophistication and the grooves will be a great home for mosses once they colonize. With this deep scoring, however, it does no good to be half-hearted. Control some of the scoring, especially around the rim, but don't be afraid to go deep at some points, or to place lines parallel and close to each other. The nature of a texture is an overall pattern, it is not a drawing, or even a repetition exactly. Work close up, but frequently step back. And walk around your piece, or turn it.

Deep texturing is not the best idea for a trough with fragile, too-thin walls. But the bigger, thicker troughs are prime for it. A wild texture can seem too big a leap—after all, you have just spent a lot of time and energy producing this vessel. But some of my best textural breakthroughs have come about after an error or even outright break-age. If a piece has broken in half, you can creatively vandalize it with impunity. If an unexpected major crease is apparent upon unmolding, go with it! Do more of what the mistake looks like in a consistent way. I'm betting the result will be worth repeating.

Leverage the trough up using the table cover.

Scoop out remaining sand.

Finish the interior.

Unmolding

Unmolding a trough from a sand mold can take place from 12 to 36 hours after molding, depending on how fast the trough is setting up. You will need to test and judge this, as described earlier with standard molds. (Small and medium-size molds are almost always ready the next day. With these sizes, it is possible and desirable to lift them straight up off the sand mold, to avoid damage to the rim.)

1. LIFT THE PLASTIC TABLE COVER. When a large trough is sufficiently set up and ready to go, lift the plastic table cover enough to get your fingers under the edge of the hypertufa trough. For massive pieces, you will need a second person to help. It can also help to mound some sand behind the mold to act as a pillow to support it as you tip the trough over.

2. TIP THE TROUGH OFF THE MOLD. Once your hands are under the edges, cautiously tip the trough off the sand mold. A lot of sand may remain inside the trough and this must be scooped out.

3. WORK ON THE RIM. Make sure the rim is properly finished.

4. FINISH AND CURE. Finally, follow the same steps outlined earlier for finishing and curing.

Tool Hygiene

A variety of trough-shaping tools.

I believe in practicing kindness to tools. They repay you for it. And I do my best to inflict this belief on anyone with whom I am working. A wire brush left overnight with half-dried curds of hypertufa stuffed inside the bristles will be worthless by the next day. Paint scrapers and the like can be resharpened, but hypertufa caked on the blades can wreak havoc on the sharpening wheel. By far, the most important items to treat with respect are the clay tools. Although clay and hypertufa are similar in composition, hypertufa is much rougher on these tools. They will only perform as well as they are treated, especially the longer you have them. It is terribly easy to lose these tools inside a pile of damp sand, concrete hardening on the blades and moisture damaging the handles.

So I baby my tools. At the end of the day, they get brought inside, scraped off, washed in warm, soapy water, dried, and oiled. Good tools are worth the price. I come from a family with a long tradition of caring for tools, going back to my grandparents. For me, it comes with the territory. Starting off a trough-shaping day with clean, sharp tools is not only easier, it allows for fine-tuned artistry. Best of all, tools cared for with love are a pleasure to work with.

A small meatball trough with tightly pruned *Santolina virens* 'Lemon Fizz', *Coryphantha sulcata,* and *Sedum acre* 'Golden Queen'.

SAND SHAPES

Making simple shapes in sand is straightforward. Moving beyond these and trying something more experimental is satisfying, but comes with challenges. I often make a miniature version of my idea, a prototype, first. Some of the bugs in creating a new form can be worked out on this smaller scale, with less investment in time, materials, and energy if things don't work out.

A kidney bean shape is probably the best for beginners to try. It won't look like a beginner's trough at all, but the shape is the most forgiving. Kidney bean troughs seem to look best when they end up asymmetrical, with one lobe bigger than the other. There are lots of variables to play with, from wall steepness to the sharpness or shallowness of the curves. Keep in mind that the cleft or indented side seems always to read as the front, so make adjustments accordingly. Ovals are organic and fun to make, but for some reason they usually want to become egg shapes. Or lemons. I have nothing against eggs or lemons, but once finished, these pieces simply don't deliver that clean, classic look of an oval.

"Meatball" troughs have walls built up using balls of hypertufa. The balls should not be perfect spheres; they always look better squashed a little. Never place one ball directly over another. The rules for building with stone and brick apply here: no joint should be directly above another joint. It weakens the structure. I've found that triangles refuse to be right triangles and slip inexorably into equilaterals. I can't really explain why. Slightly rounded triangles seem aesthetically easier to place in the garden.

It seems to be one of those quirky laws that a new idea pops up on the very last day of trough making. That day, as I unmold, I'm usually thinking, "Darn. This idea bears exploring. I could make this rounder (or taller, or smoother, or more irregular) and we will really have something." And that is why I keep "Notes for Next Year" tucked away for future use.

Lucky charms

I have a stern policy against what I call the Lucky Charm Syndrome: creating troughs in whimsical shapes. Clover leaves, hearts, sickle moons, stars, daisies—these shapes, besides often being difficult to form, can also work against your chances for success by posing problems when trying to fit roots into tight corners. And even if plants establish, they often wind up obscuring the shape anyway. Sometimes a fanciful shape is warranted, but generally, there's a reason these novelty troughs rarely sell at nurseries.

Making a Multilevel Trough with a Sand Mold

The multilevel, or pocket, trough often grabs the new trough maker's imagination. But to make one is a somewhat advanced undertaking. If you have an especially good grasp of geometry and three-dimensional spaces, it may be a perfect challenge for you. It must be approached in steps and can only be done, as far as I know, on a sand mold.

1. FORM THE MAIN, USUALLY LARGEST, LEVEL OR POCKET FIRST. A good way to start is to use a kidney shape. Make it taller than you think it needs to be, because every other level gets shorter after this one. For a two-pocket trough, you will want ten to twelve inches of height, at least. Form this sand mold as outlined for other sand molds.

2. COVER THIS MOLD WITH HYPERTUFA. Build up your trough as you would with any other sand mold. Do not apply sand to the outside, however.

3. FILL IN THE BOTTOM NOW, OR WAIT UNTIL THE SECOND POCKET IS DONE. If you fill now, poke a drainage hole into this level. Your visual reference for where you need drainage holes disappears as more levels are added; each level requires one.

4. DECIDE WHERE TO PLACE THE SECOND POCKET.

5. BUILD UP A PLATFORM OF SAND. Make it at least two, but as many as four, inches deep around the base of the hypertufa shape you have made. This measurement represents how much lower the second pocket will be from the top rim.

Begin forming a kidney shape.

A multilevel trough needs height.

The first, tallest level, or pocket.

After building a sand elevation platform and second pocket shape, score the site of attachment.

Adding the second pocket.

Bring the bottoms of both pockets to the same level.

6. BUILD THE MOLD FOR THE SECOND POCKET. Using more sand, build up a shape on top of the sand platform right up against the first hypertufa shape. This must come up as tall as the bottom you have already completed, leaving room for filling in the new bottom. Avoid scattering excess sand against the finished hypertufa walls, as this can lead to weak joins. Firm the sand pocket shape carefully without damaging the finished part.

7. LEVEL THE SAND PLATFORM. Go back and level the sand platform below as evenly and smoothly as possible. Use a flat cement trowel for a crisp edge. This is important because it will be the rim of your second pocket. I know I continually sermonize about rims. But it is one of the most immediately visible aspects of your trough. Many otherwise spectacular troughs have been flawed by a damaged rim.

8. CLEAN AWAY SAND. Brush off sand accidentally adhering to the hypertufa.

9. SCORE THE HYPERTUFA SURFACE. To strengthen the bond, score the hypertufa surface in those areas where you will be attaching the second pocket.

10. ATTACH AND BUILD THE SECOND POCKET. At each attachment site, use wetter handfuls of mix than is usual. It should not be as wet as slurry; it still needs to hold its shape and help secure the pocket to the main body. Start, laying your rim evenly.

11. BUILD THE WALLS UP IN COURSES. In the usual way, lay the hypertufa courses, being careful to achieve a good bond each time you join the second pocket to the first level or pocket. Proceed all the way up to the existing bottom of the trough.

Add the final course, extending it beyond the sand mold.

Fill bottoms with slurry.

Remember to add drainage holes.

Several lifters are needed to unmold big pieces.

12. MAKE THE WALLS HIGHER THAN THE SAND MOLD. Build walls beyond the sand mold, about one and a half inches taller. This is will be the bottom of your trough.

13. FILL IN THE BOTTOMS OF BOTH POCKETS WITH SLURRY.

14. MAKE DRAINAGE HOLES. If you didn't make one for the first pocket earlier, form drainage holes for both levels now.

15. STOP WITH ONE POCKET, OR ADD MORE. You may want to stop with one pocket. Or you can continue adding pockets to your trough in this manner until you reach a shallowness limit. Each successive level becomes shallower. The visual balance of these multilevel troughs almost always demands that the side with the shallowest pocket becomes the front. Just a hint to put your best work into that side.

16. COVER WITH PLASTIC AND LEAVE OVERNIGHT. Weight the edges with sand and allow the trough to set up overnight.

17. TEXTURE, UNMOLD, FINISH, AND CURE.

We call this the yin-yang shape. A planted yin-yang trough can be seen on page 93.

Building a Multilevel, Stonelike Trough Planter

1 Create the sand mold for the first level or pocket.

2 Keep the shape crisp while applying the hypertufa courses.

3 Build a sand platform for the second pocket and sketch its shape in the sand.

4 Lay the rim evenly and build the walls up in courses.

5 Sculpt some rocklike edges into the second pocket's walls.

6 Form an even bottom and place a drainage hole in each pocket. Cover and leave overnight. Texture the next day.

Call in back-up help for unmolding larger molds. Four (or more) hands are better able to protect the edges.

Finish the unmolded trough and cure.

Plant the trough with favorite alpines or succulents.

Backfilling to Create a Narrow-Necked Trough

Backfilling is a nifty trick for those shapes, like urns, where you want the neck to be narrower than the body of the trough. While it uses sand as a mold, it is formed inside rather than outside the mold. This is truly an advanced method, so having a bunch of experience with other forms will help with the nuances. Bear in mind that, even with this trick, if you attempt a large size, it can get difficult to the point of impossibility. About a foot tall can be handled; at a foot and a half, maintaining symmetry becomes very hard.

1. DIG A BOWL SHAPE. In a substantial pile of sand, dig a bowl shape, being careful to dig down to the flatness of the table. These vessels are constructed right-side up, so the flat table becomes the flat bottom. For an urn, expose a round space on the table surface. It's handy to use an actual bowl to settle into this nest, also helpful to pack the outside sand against it. The walls of this bowl shape should not curve inward—yet. Gravity will be angry with you. Remove the bowl if you used one.

2. LINE THE BOWL SHAPE INTERIOR WITH HYPERTUFA. Make the bottom and walls a reasonable thickness, depending on the overall size of the urn. Stop wall-building at the point you want to begin to curve inward.

3. MAKE A DRAINAGE HOLE IN THE BOTTOM. Plug this hole with damp sand to keep it open.

4. BACKFILL WITH SAND. Once the walls are at the top of the mold, it's time to add sand to the interior of the hypertufa walls. This is called backfilling. Try to keep sand from getting on the current rim of the bowl. Continue backfilling and packing down gently (remember, there is only sand holding the bowl's shape.) When you reach the bowl's rim, continue adding sand to form an interior dome above the current rim. Against this dome is where your last course or two of hypertufa will lean.

Using a form helps in creating a bowl shape.

Ready for hypertufa to start forming the bottom and walls.

Build up courses of hypertufa inside the form, only to the top of the sand mold.

The last course or two of hypertufa forms the urn's rim.

Use tools to help touch up the rim.

5. CLEAN OFF ANY ERRANT SAND. Sand on top of the current hypertufa rim will weaken the bond with the next course and promote breakage at this juncture. I also like to rewet the current rim first, and score it a little.

6. LAY THE RIM OF THE URN. This will be the final course(s) of hypertufa. It will lean inward against the sand dome inside the bowl.

7. TWEAK THINGS BEFORE THE HYPERTUFA BEGINS TO SET UP. Check the levelness and uniform thickness of the rim, even using a beveled or flat angle for the top edge. Smooth and shape the edges.

8. COVER FOR THE NIGHT, TEXTURE THE NEXT DAY, UN-MOLD, FINISH, AND CURE.

Ready to be covered until the next day.

The Concave, Right Side Up Sand Mold

Sand molds don't have to be made upside down and inside out. The mold can indeed be constructed right-side up by creating a concave depression in a pile of sand. However, in my experience, these are harder to control. They often turn out too shallow and the bottoms are hard to make flat. They are also hard to visualize as you work, because you are working blind—the outside surface of the trough is not visible to you. This is definitely a more advanced method; a technique to try after you master the others.

CRISP GEOMETRY IN SAND

Specific geometric forms are the hardest of all to make. When you think about it, the medium of hypertufa is a soft, gloppy, amoebic one. It intrinsically does not want to become a trapezoid or a chevron or a parallelogram. To accomplish such contours takes patience, finesse, and skill.

The sand for a geometrically shaped mold must be precisely the right dampness, to hold its edge and shape. The form you build must be exact; correcting a wonky line during the finishing stage is much harder in geometric forms. A hard-edged sculpture that fails at its hard edge simply fails, period.

There are a couple tricks and tools that can help while forming a tightly angled sand mold. One is to use straight boards to pack the sand against. Large rectangular cement trowels are also a big help, either to pack against, carve away uneven portions, or to pack down and make things level. They can be used as a guide for a right angle, too. (While these are good ideas for a highly angular form, using a sand mold and boards to create a simple rectangular trough seems silly, though. A modest-sized trough in this uncomplicated form can be made with a plastic rectangle or wooden mold.) Where the sand and straight board–trowel approach shines is in producing long window box–shaped troughs and baguette shapes (a long rectangle with rounded ends). Both are seriously fun to plant up. You will want a clean sand mold to start. It helps to get the hypertufa to the right moisture level as well. Shoring up with sand is useful, especially on long sides. Once the trough is molded, the surfaces can

A saturated use of red colorant in both the brick and canyon shapes. The jar rim has a touch of red. These colors beg for silver plants.

be smoothed with one of the bigger rectangular cement trowels.

Before putting one of these crisp shapes to bed for the night, I like to revisit them. If they have set up a little, edges can be sharpened up by wet carving with the blade of a knife, gently trimming and tightening the look of the outside. Don't go overboard with this, though—a too-thin wall can be the result. And by the way, I have indeed made troughs in the form of a trapezoid, a chevron, and a parallelogram. The only one that has stayed in the line-up is the chevron, under a new name: the boomerang.

VISION, ART, AND HAPPY ACCIDENTS

The art of trough making must serve the common good of the uncommon alpine plant. But this is not to suggest that following a whim, elaborating upon a happy accident, or making an impossible shape possible is not at times brilliant. Many fantastic new prototypes come about in just this way. Being open to the creative flash of a sudden idea makes the work meaningful. I've come to live with—and sometimes live by—an interesting concept: what I visualize in my mind is rarely what I end up producing. It is not a failure of vision, it is a willingness to go with inspiration, to trust what occurs between hand and medium. Art and craftsmanship are what happens within that translation.

SOIL *for* TROUGHS

THE PLANTING MEDIUM USED in containers cannot be the same as the soil in your garden. Garden loam is denser and heavier than a potting mix and doesn't drain properly in confinement. It also tends to carry pests and diseases, as well as potential weed seeds.

A major aspect of growing plants (especially alpines) in troughs is drainage. Perfect drainage is when water poured into a container seeps in quickly and through the medium, not puddling or forming quagmires that can badly affect the roots. Alpines especially abhor water pooling around their crowns. There are several ways to get this kind of drainage. One important element is the planting mix you use. There are probably as many trough soil recipes as there are rock gardeners, and no doubt there is validity to most of them. I include here the recipe I use most often; for most alpine plants in troughs, it produces a good all-purpose medium.

I provide the measurements as a ratio by volume, for simplicity. Your volume measure can be anything from a coffee can or a five-gallon bucket to a wheelbarrow. For something smaller, cut off the bottom of a clean, plastic, one-gallon jug and use that as your scoop. No need to be microscopically accurate about measuring, just use the same unit for all ingredients. Try tossing ingredients together in a large sweater box or other plastic storage bin. This also has the advantage of being sealable, storable, and portable. You can place it in your garden cart with the rest of your tools and plants, enabling you to do your plant-up right where your trough will live.

A benchful of mixed soil in the background. Small piles, clockwise from top center: pumice, coarse perlite, Turface, timed-release fertilizer. In the scoop: grit for top dressing.

Deep troughs benefit from good soil and superior drainage. The star of this planting is a beautiful twisting pine.

Trough Soil Recipe

⅔ to ¾ by volume peat-based soilless potting mix
⅓ to ¼ by volume coarse perlite
¼ by volume ¼-inch gravel (highly recommended unless weight
   is a concern)

1. **MIX THE ABOVE INGREDIENTS, IN THE STATED RATIOS.**

2. **FOR EVERY 1 GALLON OF THE ABOVE MIXTURE, ADD:**
   ¼ cup medium-grade Turface
   1 tablespoon timed-release fertilizer (if base mix does not include
      fertilizer)*

3. **BLEND ALL INGREDIENTS.** Use clean tools—dirty equipment may introduce pathogens to your mix and ruin all your hard work. If you have a tub or a wheelbarrow of mix, a small border shovel or even a large scoop or sturdy, clean dustpan will work. Since I am mixing on a big potting bench and making a large amount of soil, I use a flat-bottomed shovel with a D handle, both of which make for easier mixing.

4. **TURN THE SOIL THREE TIMES.** Intersperse a few sprays of water from a watering can or wand as necessary for dampening. An alert to make life easier down the road: peat-based soils, if allowed to dry out, can become hydrophobic, which means that they repel water instead of absorbing it. It can be fiendishly hard to rewet peat moss. Always dampen your soil while mixing, or if it has rested and dried out before you use it. If it has become powdery, a good overnight remedy is to fill a watering can with fairly hot water and slowly pour it on the peat moss. Heated water is absorbed much faster and better. Then cover the soil and leave it until the next morning. Give it a few tosses and you should have a nicely moistened potting soil for your trough.

I like to use a combination of a timed-release fertilizer and one that includes a beneficial mycorrhiza (the mycelium of a fungus that works in symbiosis with plant roots). It has proved helpful in the propagation of alpine plants and in extending the longevity of difficult subjects.

Conifers such as *Juniperus communis* 'Gold Cone' in the background of this trough can benefit from a more acidic planting medium.

TWEAKING THE MIX

This basic mix can be altered for moisture-loving plants by cutting back on the perlite. The pH can be adjusted by the kind of stone and gravel you use and by the careful addition of amendments (this information could cover a whole chapter by itself, but is easily found online and in other gardening books). Remember that your trough contains cement and will continue to leach a certain amount of lime into the soil. To acidify the planting medium for plants such as rhododendrons and conifers, you might try a mix targeted to African violets. I am reluctant to recommend using hydrated or slaked lime in any planting application, even more so for sensitive alpines.

Crocking

For many generations, gardeners believed that placing a layer of gravel, rocks, broken terra cotta, or crockery at the bottom of containers would improve drainage. The thinking was that it would increase the speed that water flowed from the denser medium of the potting soil through the more open layer at the bottom. Science has since proved this to be false and shown that it can in fact hinder the drainage. Water will flow through one medium, but it will perch when it hits a different substance or horizon in the soil. The result can be waterlogged roots. Plus, crocking makes your container that much shallower. So skip this layer when you are planting, and simply use a piece of window screen to cover the drainage holes.

I prefer to use natural versions such as oyster shells or small pieces of dolomitic limestone. The same goes for the harsher sulfur and ferrous sulfur to boost acidity. Go gentle with these roots—they can be easily burned. It is always best to have the medium tested before applying pH-altering elements.

Depending on your goals and climate, the addition of pumice can be a magic bullet for hard-to-grow alpines. As little as a tenth by volume will make a real difference, and for extra-tricky plants, you can use as much as a third by volume. Get the real McCoy: coarse grade, unwashed, and not kilned. (Avoid the man-made stand-ins.) You want the gritty particles known as "fines" that coat the pumice particles. And you don't want every molecule of moisture cooked out of them, as is done for some building purposes. Silver saxifrages respond especially well to pumice in soil mixes, as do western penstemons and the loco weeds such as astragalus and oxytropis. The addition of pumice (and gravel, too, for that matter) helps keep the structure of your soil mix viable longer. Over time, every potting mix becomes denser, less aerated, and muckier. But the quarter-inch gravel and pumice help slow down this process, leaving you with a better soil structure for a longer amount of time.

By the way, if earthworms have somehow gotten into your trough, this is not a positive thing. Though they are dependable fertilizers and aerators of garden soil, they can wreak havoc inside alpine troughs. The breakdown of the soil structure will happen much sooner. Even worse, they don't distinguish between a fragment

of decomposing matter and small thread-like roots, devouring both as they move through the soil. The other unwanted outcome is soil that's too rich for the taste of mountain plants.

A good planting mix and excellent drainage are especially crucial in large troughs such as this, which is four feet across at its rim.

PERFECT DRAINAGE

Perfect drainage means that the roots have plenty of air around them, in the tiny interstitial spaces in the soil once the water has drained away. Because drainage is about the flow of water, I have come to believe that it is very much tied to a container's shape and depth, not just the mix inside. A tall pot or a raised wall or berm will always drain better than something of lesser depth. To test this concept, simply hold a sponge of uniform density flat on your upward-facing palm and slowly begin to pour water onto it. Stop before it trickles out. Then turn the sponge vertically and very quickly the water will start draining out. Turn the sponge flat again and it will abruptly stop. Now picture your trough and imagine the soil inside it as the sponge in your hand. For sharp drainage, deeper is always better.

Don't be tempted to add sand to your soil mix to improve drainage—it most often will have the opposite effect. Unless your mix consists of fifty percent sand or more, sand will make it denser and wetter. Imagine you are making a big vat of pasta salad for a picnic. You have a gallon of cooked pasta shells and decide to add a quart of peas. When you have combined the two, do you have a gallon plus a quart of salad? You do not, because the peas are inside the pasta. The same thing happens with large aggregates in soil combined with something much smaller. One fits inside the other, locking up air space that is so precious to plant roots and creating more tiny surface areas on which a wet film can adhere. The exception to this is including much larger chunks, such as quarter-inch gravel (or even larger), which will actually hasten moisture flow, creating pathways around the chunks. Win the battle for perfect drainage, and the outlook for happy alpines is pretty good.

PLANTING YOUR TROUGH

To the uninitiated, troughs are an enigma, the skill to design and plant them unaccountably out of reach. People who are perfectly competent gardeners in all other ways seem timid about stepping into this project without help. It is useful to remember that this is, after all, just another garden—only smaller. It will function under the same laws of nature and will benefit just as much from aesthetic prowess.

What follows are some fundamental plant-up steps, focusing on the classic miniature landscape. All these steps are applicable to simpler plantings, too. More ways to get creative can be found in the chapter on planting styles.

Planting Basics

1. ASSESS PLANTING DEPTH. Your empty trough should have enough depth to keep alpine roots happy. A plant that might fit under a coffee cup above ground can have far-ranging roots as long as a yard or more. What is an adequate depth? It all depends on what will be growing in the trough and for how long. A shallow pan trough four inches deep or less is only good at keeping succulents happy. Honestly, even they will display more vibrancy when given a little extra depth. It is possible to keep many different species content for the span of one season in a shallow vessel, as long as there

Pruned conifer fronted by *Draba rigida* in bloom.

is some lateral room for the roots to go and the winter is not too punishing. But in a short time, occupants run the risk of becoming starved. If the lateral room for roots to run is also limited, the problem worsens. The last thing you want to do with a small, shallow container is to plant root-thugs such as the thymes and many varieties of conifers, or anything with dense, fibrous roots. Six inches or more of inside depth and a width of twelve inches give you a wider range of choices. My ideal trough is at least eight inches deep.

2. CONFIRM AND COVER DRAINAGE HOLES. Before planting a trough, if you did not make it yourself, check to see that it has one or more holes of adequate size in the bottom. If there are no holes, they will have to be drilled. The number will depend on the size of the trough. A twelve-inch-square (or round) trough can do with one. If the trough is a long one, like a window box, there should be a drainage hole every six or seven inches down the length. The diameter of the hole should be somewhere between three-quarters of an inch and one and a half inches. Any smaller, and it can become clogged. Prepare the trough by covering drainage holes with screening material. A favorite is the synthetic screen used for windows that can be bought by the foot or yard at any hardware store. It is easily cut to fit with scissors. You can just place a patch over the hole or cover the entire bottom with screening.

3. ADD THE SOIL MIX RECIPE YOU CREATED. Pile in your beautiful, aerated, lightly moistened soil. Gently, using all ten fingers pointing down, tamp the soil a little. Never compact soil, as the air it holds is as essential for healthy roots as are the nutrients the soil contains. The soil level in your trough will depend on whether you plan to create earthworks or level changes inside the trough (more on these shortly). If the planting will be on one level, fill to the rim of the trough, realizing there will be settling, which is normal.

4. DECIDE WHAT TYPE OF PLANTING WILL BE BEST FOR YOUR TROUGH. The most classic look in a trough planting is that of the miniature landscape. Success is dependent on small, authentic details, ultimately promoting a suspended disbelief, convincing you of this smaller world. Some components of a miniature landscape include a shrub or anchor plant, a few handsome stones, perhaps a ground cover, buns and cushions, a succulent, and maybe something charming drooling picturesquely over the edge.

Synthetic window screening has been cut to fit the bottom of the trough, covering the drainage holes to prevent soil loss.

However, creating a landscape in a container requires the elbow room to pull it off. Scale is paramount, as is the trough's shape. A landscape is traditionally a horizontal thing, wider than it is tall. So if you are planting in a trough that is taller than it is wide, or in a small trough (less than twelve inches in diameter), pursuing a landscape inside that small surface area may not be practical. If that is the case, proceed to step 7 now.

But if your trough's size and shape is large enough to accommodate a mini landscape, now is the time—while you're filling your trough with soil—to play with earthworks a little. It is so much more interesting to have a level change in this tiny geography.

Mound up a substantially larger quantity of soil in a given quadrant. It can be a quarter, even two-thirds of your planting surface, whatever feels right. Just don't split the real estate half and half; that would read as not having movement or the good kind of visual tension. Tamp down lightly, then add more soil to the elevated section if needed.

5. EMPLOY STONES. It is almost always helpful to employ rocks to buttress and contain the soil, and to help replicate rocky landscapes. You can procure rocks by purchasing them from landscape materials companies or perhaps collecting them on your own land. You may want to bury a piece of stone or two (not your prettiest ones) underneath more showy stones, to support a level change and to mitigate settling later. Don't be afraid to include a substantial number of stones, but use only one sort of stone per trough.

Try not to dot them around the space evenly. Think in clusters and outriders. As you go about creating a realistic outcrop, you are often actually creating more areas to plant in the wedge of soil between the rocks. Be fearless about creating height with rock, as long as a stabilizing portion of that rock is below the ground.

As you do this, face what will be the front, or the best side of the trough. Of course, you may be planning to display the piece in the round, visible from all sides. If this is the case, work on it on a small table or counter that you can circle as you place the plants. Even then, I am willing to bet there is a dominant face: the side you see upon entering the garden, maybe, or from the living room window. It is also good to keep in mind the height of the final display site. Will it be viewed from eye level, table level, or the ground? The orientation of your design should take this into account.

Use the same quality of attention while examining your stones as you do for your plants. Move them around together, find interesting faces or the way they will fit together best. After forming a major outcrop, it can be pleasing to place a couple of smaller rocks farther out, as though there is another, deeper buried beak of the same rock outcrop.

If you're someone who firmly abjures shrubs or woody plants of any kind in a trough, consider using just an outcrop of stone as your anchor. Let it rise substantially, and place it to the side and toward the back a little. Never be afraid to make something massive, relatively speaking. Avoid bittyness and be bold. Devising an outcrop with uptilt is highly effective both visually and culturally. Your choices

Think about using support rocks to shore up a level change.

Don't be afraid to use several large rocks to create an outcrop.

Using more than one type of rock never works.

run from absolutely perpendicular to the not-quite-horizontal. As you move into the more horizontal, though, pay attention to how water will run over the rocks. Will any flow into the root zones of plants that you have sandwiched between stones? An overhanging shelf can create an unintended dry patch beneath it. This may be a blessing for some species, anathema to others.

Consider building a high point like a mesa—flatter, but raised up—and contrive to have planting areas around or beside it. For even more drama, create a gorge directly below it. These sorts of earthworks often look best when they are set at least partly on the diagonal inside the footprint of the trough. Larger stone crevices and the walls of a gorge need some underpinning of support with other stones beneath them; don't simply plop stones on top of the soil. They will sink after a couple waterings and your design will sink out of sight, too.

A successful vertical outcrop, with one type of rock.

Rocks built into an imposing crevice can function as the trough's anchor.

6. CHOOSE AND POSITION AN ANCHOR PLANT. If you are using an anchor plant, position it now. It is always a good idea to work with the anchor plant and stones at the same time—if one needs to shift, generally the other does, too. A shrub or conifer looks wonderfully natural snugged up against a big, significant stone. Do not place an anchor plant perfectly dead center; it will subtract from any visual dynamic you may be creating.

And before you plant the small tree or shrub, turn it around and examine its character on all sides. Choose the best face, or create it. Now is the time to prune up a few limbs, open up a little space, even begin to prune for a lean, windswept look. For windswept, it will probably take more than one pruning session in more than one season. And you must decide which direction the so-called wind will be coming from, to make this work. I find it often helps to prune off all twigs, tips, and needles from the underside of each branch. But work slowly, taking time now and then to assess your cuts. Better to stop and come back to this later than to rush ahead.

At this point, you have committed to three important things: the shape (and thus the character) of your trough, the personality of your anchor plant, and a category of stone. This is the moment your trough planting begins to acquire a soul. So much of what your trough will become is cradled inside these choices. A shrub and stones are your biggest elements. Get these balanced now. Your decisions have already guided you into a style. Follow that.

7. MAKE SURE THE PLANTING HOLE IS BIG ENOUGH. I usually use a few fingers to dig the hole for my trough plants, taking care to look at the volume of the roots and then to allow enough space for the roots to spread laterally and downward. You can also use a small crevice trowel or an old kitchen spoon.

8. CRADLE THE PLANT AND POT UPSIDE DOWN. There's a trick to releasing plants from their nursery pots. There's no need to pound the bottom of the pot with a trowel, or yank and twist the plant to free it. Check that there are no roots growing through the

Juniperus chinensis 'Shimpaku', pruned on the left, unpruned on the right. Pruning can substantially change the tone and style of the entire garden.

holes in the bottom of the pot. If there are, trim them. It is kinder to clip any that are tangled.

Place your index and middle fingers on either side of the stem if it is a single-stemmed plant. If it is a cushion or mound, firmly but delicately cup your hand over the foliage and turn it upside down. Rap the edge or the corner of the pot sharply downward against a table edge, bench, even a rock or step. It should take only one or two raps for the plant to be free.

9. CAREFULLY REMOVE THE TOP LAYER OF SOIL AROUND THE PLANT. This is one of the best tips I've ever learned. The top layer is where every weed seed will be located, whether you purchased the plant at the finest nursery or it was a gift. You can drastically cut down on the introduced weeds in your garden by discarding this exposed layer. Beyond trough plants, this is a good idea for any new planting, from an annual passed over the hedge from a neighbor to a big balled and burlapped shrub from a garden center.

10. UNTANGLE THE SOIL FROM THE ROOT BALL. Using a pencil, chopstick, or your fingers, begin to tease out and untangle the soil from the bottom of the root ball upward. If you work patiently, you will feel the root ball loosen up. I do not strictly adhere to bare-rooting the plant (although many alpine experts do), preferring to treat the roots a bit more gently. This decision is dependent on your assessment of the soil in the root ball compared to your trough soil. Ideally, they should be close in content and structure. You want the roots to unfurl and permeate the soil in their new home. If you choose to bare root the plant, timing is essential: do not leave the roots exposed to heat or sun, and get them into the soil quickly. Another tip is to perform this untangling while the roots are on the dry side. Roots seem to get much more damaged when teased out wet.

Three 'Shimpaku' junipers, pruned and planted against a rock outcrop.

11. PLACE THE PLANT IN THE HOLE. Roots grow in three dimensions, so when nestling roots into the soil, spread them out gently in different directions, making sure they are not bunched up in a clump. Hold the plant above the hole by its stem or leaves, lower it in and backfill with soil as the roots dangle into their home. Once settled into place, the plant needs the soil level brought back up to what it was in the pot. A tree or shrub will bear visible evidence of the original soil level on the surface of its trunk (check this while planting). Once the plant is in place, don't firm the roots too much—just a light pressure with three fingers of both hands around the stem. I rely on the watering-in to eliminate air pockets and to tamp the soil into place. The one exception is gentians, which prefer to be planted firmly.

Do your best not to crowd plants. I know this is not always avoidable. Sometimes the design makes us thrust two plants close together, or up against a rock or the side of the trough. All I stress is that you try to preserve the viability of the roots as you plant. And, in point of fact, many, if not most plants are happy in the company of others, and pretty much every one of them adores the cool presence of stone.

Antennaria 'McClintock' makes a good underplanting.

12. SELECT AND INSTALL UNDERPLANTINGS. A nice effect beneath an anchor specimen is a ground cover. Planting this will take a little finesse. At the same time you are settling in the anchor planting, select a potful or two of a flat ground cover that does not seem too rootbound. You will want to loosen the roots substantially. Cutting a slit through the mat is another effective maneuver. First, tease out the roots, then make the cut and work it around the trunk or stem, like a skirt around the base of a Christmas tree. If done with care, you can achieve an almost instant effect. The finesse comes in gauging how thick the root mat is on the teased-out ground cover, and how much depth the base of the tree will accept. We are working in fractions of an inch here.

Lay down ground cover in the miniature landscape.

Firm things in gently. If you can afford more time for the ground cover to get established, or, if you have encountered a stubbornly solid root ball on an anchor plant, try tucking in small plugs of ground cover divided out from a larger plant. Early in the season is

Add cushions.

the best time for this. Another big advantage of these little ground covers is erosion control on slopes and levels of the earthworks.

Evaluate your design midway. Are the stones at a good and believable angle? Are they consistent? Is the anchor plant settled in naturally and showing off its best face? Is it tilted? Should it be tilted? Now is a time to make adjustments.

13. ADD THE REST OF THE GEMS. Look over your assemblage of plants. Select for complementary or contrasting texture, color, and form in foliage. Remember, blooms in general and alpine blooms in particular are a flash in the pan. Get excited by other inherent qualities of the plants. If your conifer is blue-green, do you want blue foliage to be a theme? Or you may want to contrast its cool color with a vibrant yellow.

Foliage color as a theme in a trough can be beautiful and brilliant. One of my very favorite plant-ups was dedicated to silver and burgundy foliage. Many pale gray and silver plants were combined with some rich red succulents, the dark burgundy leaves of *Armeria maritima* 'Rubrifolia', some terra-cotta–colored stones, and reddish gravel. Potent drama and not a flower in sight. Play with plant textures, too: a shiny reflective leaf near a velvety one, tiny tight leaves against a smooth rock, or cascading foliage chaining down the rough side of the trough.

Before planting your remaining alpines, move them around in the spaces not yet occupied. Switch things, test them out. Often one plant will demand to be in the front corner, another is only comfortable toward the back, maybe next to a stone. Irises are famous for (visually) demanding stone near them, it is simply a perfect match. Don't be afraid to leave unoccupied spaces in your design. All landscapes have them. More than that, all good landscapes depend on empty spaces, areas of calm. Think about what a sweep of emerald lawn does for a large design. By overstuffing a trough, you turn it into any old container planting.

If you have created a gorge with rocks, carpet it with the flattest, lowest ground cover you can. Remember, an inch may not seem like much, but an inch of plant height in your trough might half fill your gorge, stealing the drama. I would pick a single species to line the gorge, and not confuse things with varying textures. Obey nature. In the wild, we always find the sere and brown or tough gray and silver plants surviving up on that windy tableland. In the moister swale, you find lush emerald and chartreuse. An example of a planted gorge can be seen on page 156.

How you space the plants is important, too. If you simply space plants evenly around the container, there will be no dynamic interest, no tension. Cluster two or three plants, allow blanks for breathing room, add one or two against a rock or the far trough wall. This is the magic moment, the moment when things fall into place. If they don't, shuffle things around a little, or exchange something for a plant you never thought would work—it might surprise you by being the perfect element. If there is nothing ideal for a spot you want to fill, here's a radical idea: be brave. Plan to leave a gap, for a selection to be named later. It's a great excuse to comb the catalogs or visit your favorite nursery.

When stuck, one rather obvious solution is doubling (or tripling) up on plants already used. Would that ground cover texture read as lawn if you used three plants? Or consider a cushion in a largish size, with another, much smaller one, nearby. What about filling in a whole crevice between two rocks with multiples of the same succulent, or a line of tiny acorus?

When you are satisfied with plant placement, unpot as described previously. Use your fingers to cajole the plants into their spots. Keep them at roughly the depth they were in their nursery pots. As you plant, if you have built level changes in the trough, pay attention to keeping the high places high and the low sites low. Walk around the whole trough occasionally to check that things look balanced, especially from the major face, or front.

14. GENTLY SWEEP. When all your plants are in place, it is time to pull out the most high-tech device you will be using: the dust brush. Some prefer the whisk broom shape; I have always liked the soft ones shaped like a giant toothbrush. A new soft paintbrush also works nicely. It is important to brush things off before mulching the trough. Otherwise, bits of perlite will end up on top of the mulch. It is true that you can't entirely prevent perlite from floating

Once you've finished planting, carefully sweep excess soil and perlite from rocks and crevices, away from woody trunks, and off other plants.

Mulch (or grit) with small gravel.

Brush lightly again after gritting.

up altogether, but this step will keep it to a minimum. Gently and carefully sweep the soil and perlite away from trunks, off the tiny ground cover and the cushions. Disentangle any debris caught in a trailer. Be painstaking in brushing off all crevices in your rockwork, too. And finish by sweeping the brush along all the trough edges to clear them.

15. MULCH, OR GRIT, THE SURFACE. Apply stone grit or small gravel generously to the soil surface. Don't even think about using an organic mulch such as wood chips or shredded anything unless you are doing a completely woodland trough. Alpines hate organic mulch. It creates moisture at the crown, something to be avoided with mountain plants. Stone mulches perform more than an aesthetic job; they also keep the soil cool and the crowns of plants dry. Mulch wherever there is bare soil showing. Then brush everything down again, gently.

16. GARNISH AFTER GRITTING. Sometimes even after settling in the rocks, planting, and gritting, there is still a sense that something is missing. A small detail or two, something to add complexity or richness. I occasionally add a few buttons of an interesting sempervivum or a couple of sprigs of a gray sedum. Succulents lend themselves to this, agreeing to root easily. It is best to do this after you mulch; otherwise you may bury them too deep (they are only small cuttings) and, believe it or not, this method results in less mess as you are finishing up.

Look at the little spot you want to garnish. Then choose accordingly. A large rosette might be loaded with drama but could throw off your hard-won scale. You can use this as an opportunity to reinforce foliage color

Separate rosettes from their nursery pot.

Use a pencil or other narrow tool to help make planting holes for small succulent garnishes.

A secret rosette can be a lovely surprise on the backside of a trough garden.

schemes, or to contrast them. There are so many tonalities available, from the white webbing of *Sempervivum arachnoideum*, to rose and blush colors, reds, grays, and a spectrum of greens to almost blue. This kind of subtle surprise lends opulence to the entire planting.

17. MOVE THE TROUGH TO ITS GARDEN LOCATION AND WATER. Always place the trough in its permanent home before you water. I plan beforehand where the trough will go and have the area ready. Then, when planting is done, I move the trough swiftly into place and water in the plants. It is no fun to have to lift a soaked, much heavier, dripping, draining trough and waddle it into place. If it's going to be a two-man lift, even dry, arrange for help at the proper moment. Or plan to plant it in place.

If the sun is particularly punishing that day or week, consider shading the trough for a few days. Shading can be anything from a table (not clear glass or plastic) to a portable lawn chair or a cut branch full of foliage positioned to thwart the most intense sun. Place it to the south or west, generally.

The trough shown on the bottom right of page 73, in which rocks were placed to create a crevice, here planted and thriving. *Saxifraga* 'Southside Seedling' tops the crevice, *Artemisia caucasica* flows down in a river of silver-green. The yellow pom-pom flowers of an eriogonum bloom on the left, *Orostachys spinosa* is below. *Saxifraga* 'Tumbling Waters' is on the right, and the small round dome in front is *Gypsophila aretioides*.

Watering in the new plantings is the final step in planting up your trough.

Months later, a lithodora has been added in the foreground.

There's a right way to water. Always have a fine rose on the end of your watering wand or on your watering can. It should mimic gentle rain. Never turn on a hose directly over your trough. Air in the hose and the resultant explosive sputtering will destroy your planting. Even the first "glug" out of a watering can may scatter mulch, dig a hole, or dislodge a rosette. Tilt the can beside the trough, then move it over the trough smoothly. Water your trough in easy sweeps with a back and forth movement. Take frequent breaks to watch the water seep in. It is often more effective to water several times lightly rather than flood everything in one shot, which can cause soil and perlite to float up and dislodge small plants. Once the trough starts draining freely, you are done.

PLACING TROUGHS
in the GARDEN

THERE IS AN ART to placing troughs to take advantage of the effect they have in the garden. They invite intimate inspection. Magnifying this effect are the little inhabitants. They beg for attention because they are close-up plants, small, gemlike, often intricate.

Before placement, take a little tour of your yard and garden. A curve in a path may be a promising spot; a trough could be elevated on a flat-topped stone to lend prominence.

Troughs atop walls are a natural; the same goes for broad (or not-so-broad) outdoor steps. Troughs can even be repeated on several steps. In a case like this, it is usually more harmonious to select one shape to use, though it is charming to vary the size—three graduated rectangles, or a set of cylinders or bowls.

A popular spot for a trough is a tabletop. Always be sure the furniture can handle the weight and will not become damaged. Watering is a fact of life, so the table must survive watering. Hypertufa, like the concrete it contains, will scratch surfaces. To protect the longevity of the trough, it should not be left elevated on a table for the winter.

Rock gardeners naturally place troughs directly into the rock garden. Many such gardens contain slopes or stairs, walls, rockwork, gorges, boulders, and expanses of gravelly scree.

Even broken troughs can be used with ingenuity on a slope. If a side is missing on a rectangle, or a bowl has split in half, bury the broken side by abutting it up against the hill, perhaps level it on the front end a bit

Troughs are set directly into a rock garden in bloom. Above, *Delosperma ashtonii* 'Blut' is in flower. Below, *Campanula chamissonis* blooms. *Erigeron scopulinus*, with little daisies, is on the ground in front.

83

Above: Decorate your steps.

Right: A rocklike trough planted with *Scabiosa japonica* var. *alpina* 'Ritz Blue', *Lewisia longipetala* 'Little Raspberry', and *Sedum* 'Borchii Sport'.

Take advantage of
a curve in a path.

Bad Places for Troughs

There actually are plenty of wrong places to locate a trough. Don't place one on a sea wall that gets regularly slapped by the ocean. (I have actually had queries about this.) Putting an alpine-filled trough anywhere indoors (that is not a cold greenhouse) will kill the plants. You may think at first that things are going well, but these are mountain plants, they react badly to coddling. Give them a life outdoors year-round. Don't position a trough right next to a built-in grill that gets really hot. Anywhere in a driveway is a bad choice. I have heard stories of troughs in all these places—and their sad outcomes.

Top: Set into a rock garden, a boat-shaped trough features *Thuja occidentalis* 'Primo', *Artemisia caucasica*, and *Lewisia longipetala* 'Little Raspberry' in flower. The cushion on the right is *Silene acaulis* 'Heidi'. Above in the jar are *Scabiosa japonica* var. *alpina* 'Ritz Blue', *Erigeron leiomerus*, and *Lewisia longipetala* 'Little Mango'.

Bottom left and right: Two halves of a broken bowl snugged against a rock face. Once planted, the two halves make a charming repetition.

with some stone flakes and pieces. This trick can be used in any setting that has a slope or a retaining wall.

A collection of troughs can set the tone and stage, giving visitors a preview of what is to come as they thread their way into the larger expanse of the garden. Troughs make a great transition, no matter what type of garden lies beyond. They serve as a gatekeeper between the more refined and architectural parts near the house, to wilder areas farther out. Set one on either of a gate, line up a few window box shapes on the far side of the pool, place a clutch together at the base of a focal point tree. They can even be used as problem solvers. At the bottom of many trees we find dry, fibrous, root-laced soil—not an easy place to get much to thrive. A few troughs around tree bases can turn a defect into a beauty spot. Are there gnarly roots in the area? Use them! A collection of small urns or cylinders look magical tucked into the torturous sculpture of exposed roots by the bole of an ancient tree.

ELEVATING TROUGHS

Many troughs benefit both aesthetically and culturally by being elevated. They drain better (as long as you are careful about not blocking the drainage holes) and they often look better in the landscape. As pedestrian an element as a gray cement block can work as a pedestal, providing you flip it so the holes don't show and the trough shape agrees with the block. If less height is appropriate, try bricks or even half bricks. Tuck them back under the bottom edge of the trough for a clean look.

With or without some sort of plinth underneath them, troughs should appear level.

Among the roots, troughs add interest to the base of this *Metasequoia glyptostroboides*.

These bases can be positioned in many cases so they are invisible and the trough appears to float above the ground. Small pieces of slate can work, too, if they are all the same thickness; they blend in well with gray tones. Clay flue liners, which come in hollow squares, rounds, and rectangles, and many heights, can be used beautifully, especially to raise a trough well off the ground. If the trough is to be set into an area of ground cover, it should be raised above the sea of plants. If you happen to have a spare empty trough of the right size, why not invert that and use it as a base? These have the advantage of being made of the same material, so they blend in well. Although the plants don't actually require leveling to grow well, a tilted trough will cause the viewer (and the gardener) to feel uneasy. It doesn't have to be engineer perfect, but it should feel balanced and level to the eye. Check from all angles before calling the job done.

Vary the heights within a multiple-trough grouping

Skillfully elevating one or two troughs makes a big difference, regardless of whether the grouping is made up of repeated shapes or a mixture of them. Even a collection of three rectangles of different sizes will look vastly more interesting if you graduate the heights, placing the highest in the back. Be bold with shapes. Combine a tall square with a short, tubby urn, then finish with a free-form or kidney shape. The ideal way to tackle this is by moving several shapes and sizes around in the space until the arrangement pleases you. How you arrange the shapes helps determine the placement of plants inside them. It becomes clear where an upright will look good, where a cascading plant belongs. Wait to plant until you have figured out the arrangement.

ADDING IN-GROUND PLANTS AROUND TROUGHS

To enhance a collection of troughs, consider adding some plantings in the ground around the trough bases. This has to be done with grace and a little restraint. It is easy to achieve on a gravel surface, but it's possible even on a paved patio (and more interesting, I think), especially if you remove a few pavers strategically.

When selecting pavers, bricks, or stones to remove from around the bases of the troughs, try for asymmetry and randomness. Don't simply lift bricks evenly all around each trough. Take out three around one corner, a stray one or two farther away, a couple between the troughs. These spots will have to be treated as little rock gardens; you must provide sharp drainage and a good root run for the plants. But you are already way ahead of the game where cultural requirements are concerned. The plant roots, as they insinuate under the paving, find the perfect cool environment in which to flourish. Think about mixing up the plant shapes and textures: a few cushions, a patch of gentians, even a decorative clump of dwarf iris, with their swordlike leaves.

There is a slight edge of decadence about this effect, a nod to the English folly, the created ruin. It borrows a dose of antiquity, as though the stones went missing ages ago and a few alpines artlessly seeded down, or a thyme drooled down far enough to touch the crack between stones and take root. Call it benign neglect, or, at least, the orchestrated appearance of it.

As the troughs are being arranged, consider the use of an upright or rounded shrub as part of the group. A daphne would be an unexpected touch. If using shrubs, choose only the smallest and slowest-growing species. Alternatively, hunt out the most glorious lichened sculptural stone you can find, and choose one large enough to have an impact. Place that in lieu of a shrub, or added to an arrangement of them.

Making repetition work for you

Repetition is a time-honored trick in all forms of gardening. Here is another truly juicy way to use it. Encourage the appearance of serendipity in the guise of self-seeding. If a *Draba rigida* lives in one corner of a trough, plant another in the ground directly below that corner. Maybe even place a few smaller ones as outliers beyond that. Almost any plant featured in troughs can be reiterated in a crack or missing paver below. If you like to let nature take its course, use some reliable self-seeders. These include many aquilegias, the drabas, arenarias, chaenorhinums, and erigerons to name a few candidates. *Erinus alpinus*—in several color forms, from white to purple to a magnetic cerise—is a real winner in this category. If you're worried about invasive self-sowing, be brave. These are just alpines, not mugwort or bishop's weed. Let them sow. Then go ahead and remove all but the perfectly placed ones you want to keep.

SUN

Although alpines crave intense sunlight, they don't like the humidity that often accompanies sun at lower elevations. Nor will they appreciate the warm nights some summers bring. Look for spots that may be sunny but a bit cooler. There may be a place where a breeze is flowing most of the time. A northwest exposure, especially if it is on a slope, can spell success when you have otherwise failed. Consider the points of the compass. South means heat, north is cool. A western aspect can cook a plant, whereas eastern sun is less intense. As far as siting goes, don't give up on a particular plant until you have failed three times in three different spots. I have on occasion placed three of the same species: one where I am sure it will thrive, one where I doubt it will be happy, and one where I'm sure it can't survive. Sometimes the last spot is where it flourishes.

Trough gardens, intermingled with shrubs and underplanting.

This yin-yang trough is planted with sun-lovers: chamaecyparis, *Delosperma alpinum*, *Armeria caespitosa* 'Red Faery', two 'Highland Cream' thyme plants, and *Penstemon linarioides* subsp. *coloradoensis*.

DEGREES OF SHADE

There is simply no shade in the mountains above timberline, so true high alpines really don't exist for shade. Therefore, if your trough is going to be in a shady location, the only palette of plants you have to choose from is a cobbled-together assortment of the tiniest shade plants that will remain in scale. There will be no rock-hard cushions, nothing gleamingly silver or bright gray. The flowers are often less brazen, too, tending toward white, softer pinks, and lavenders, with the occasional yellow tossed in. Think of the blooms on violets, thalictrums, and cymbalarias. These will be just about finished flowering when spring is over.

If the shade in your garden is caused by trees, then selective thinning, pruning, and limbing up, especially on the south side of the garden, can do a world of good to bring light in. If the trees must remain as they are, then turn this druidic proclivity into an asset! Hunt down the adorable, most miniature hostas—many carry a gold or cream variegation that will light up a shadier spot. *Hosta* 'Pandora's Box' is a beauty. Look for chartreuse tones as well; some gold leaves turn this color when grown in less light. I often prefer it to the hotter color. *Acorus gramineus* 'Minimus Aureus' is

Hosta 'Mighty Mouse', *Asplenium trichomanes*, and *Acorus gramineus* 'Minimus Aureus' are good choices for this shade trough.

a lovely grasslike plant that does this; it will provide the thin, strappy leaf to offset other foliage forms. As you mix and play with shade foliage, it sometimes becomes evident that combining too many types of variegated plants in the same container can look busy. Some stripes and patterns actually clash with others. Step back and ponder your combinations. Keep in mind that some plants are shade loving (think ferns and hostas), while others are only shade tolerant. That means they will grow passably well but you will be losing something. Some veronicas and campanulas will consent to grow in part shade but may fall out of character and will usually flower less. Some will notoriously lean toward the light source, so leaning had better be part of the plan.

Because a shade trough cannot depend as much on dramatic foliage color con-trasts, and because the plants will be leafier than the tight cushions in full sun, it pays to select an arrangement that maximizes plant differences. A conifer that tends to-ward blue-green can be happily combined with a mini hosta that features chartreuse

Troughs usually look great in close proximity to hardscape.

leaves. Or a white-flowered plant like *Hutchinsia alpina* can be highlighted with the tiny variegated white and green leaf of *Hosta* 'Cameo'. *Thalictrum kiusianum*, the smallest of the meadow rues, is lovely and low in a shade trough, with lilac flowers hovering above the leaves in late spring and early summer.

A few final words on planting up a shade trough. A shady site is serene if not downright demure. Try to bring forward some excitement. One way to do this is to select a bold, unusual, or big trough at the outset. The next step is theatrical placement in the landscape. Raise it up, isolate it in a bare area, use whatever sleight of hand you can think of to lure the eye. Within the trough itself, heighten the impact with strategic editing. Resist the urge to stuff the trough with greenery that will blend into a leafy background. Select plants with strong shapes and foliage color that will contrast. And be choosy about your stones: make them big, bold, and interesting. Leave some tranquil areas. Do yourself the favor of not relying on flowers, though you will have them, too. Fall in love, instead, with everything else.

GENUINE TUFA ROCK *and* HOW TO USE IT

REAL TUFA STONE IS a naturally occurring substance that rock gardeners have come to treasure. For many trough gardeners, it is the ultimate stone. It has root-friendly characteristics that trough makers try to mimic with hypertufa. If you are fortunate enough to acquire some of the real thing, here are a few ideas about how to use it.

Natural tufa usually forms in freshwater seeps and streams that contain a lot of suspended solids, mostly mineral, but especially calcium carbonate. Over time, the solids precipitate out of the liquid and form coatings of crystals over organic material such as shreds of moss, twigs, and leaf litter—eventually forming limestone. If you have ever watched rock candy crystals being formed on a string, it is something like that. Once the organics have rotted, dissolved, and washed away, what is left is tufa. Its internal structure is like a sponge, with many holes of different sizes. Iron oxide can make it red or yellow, and it is common to find tufa with embossed fossils. The stone is very porous and easy to carve when first dug. After being exposed to the air for a season or two, it becomes much more brittle and hard. Finding a source for tufa is often difficult. Sometimes the pieces available are much too big to fit in a normal-sized trough. They can be broken with a mallet or a cold chisel. There can be losses, though; pieces don't always break along lines you had planned and there can be some crumbling. The best thing to do is to work with the pieces atop a sheet of heavy mil plastic, to capture any fines, rubble, and tufa dust. These fines are a valuable ingredient for use around the roots of choice plants.

A variety of alpine plants growing and blooming in real tufa.

97

Alpine plants love to have their roots next to, under, and even *inside* tufa rock.

There are three basic ways to use this special kind of rock in a trough: simply as attractive elements to complement plantings; when drilled, as a root-friendly home for finicky baby alpine plants; and by sandwiching the tufa with clay and young plants to create a crevice garden within a trough.

TUFA AS A BEAUTIFUL AND BENEFICIAL STONE ELEMENT

The easiest way to use tufa is to simply treat it as a handsome rock component of your trough planting. For the benefit of plant roots, bury enough of the stone to have a positive impact on them. Shoot for about three to four inches underground, or 20 to 30 percent of the stone(s). More is even better. Since there is rarely any true striation in this rock, it provides a certain freedom to design. The rocks look natural puzzle-pieced together.

As with any stones in a container, if you are using more than one, avoid placing them at equidistant intervals. The only time I suspend this rule is with a long window box shape, where deliberate repetition can be part of the master plan. It makes sense to place the heaviest, biggest end of the tufa downward. Even in this case, though, I try not to be too predictable in placement. Cluster a couple rocks together, but leave a gap for plants. For best results, determine the placement before beginning to plant. Fill the trough with soil, then situate interesting chunks of tufa until the arrangement pleases you. Then place the plants. From this point, proceed as with any plant-up. Remember to brush off the tufa thoroughly before mulching and watering in the plants, since the texture of the rock tends to trap debris.

Moss has a special affection for tufa. In dry, sunny, exposed sites, moss may not appear, but in most other sites it tends to colonize. I have two large bowl troughs flanking a set of steps; the troughs contain only large hunks of tufa. The only plants are mosses on the tufa. From a design standpoint, I don't know that I could have done any better than letting nature take its course.

DRILLING AND PLANTING TUFA

No other stone comes close to real tufa as a welcoming bed for roots. The simple description of this method is to drill a hole and plant an alpine in it. But naturally

Drilling into real tufa stone placed within a hypertufa trough, to create spaces for plants.

there are fine points to the process. I heard a story once that an alpine enthusiast had grown some bun or cushion to a rather large size directly in a big specimen of tufa. At some point, he decided to slice the stone in half. What it revealed was the incredible extent to which the roots had penetrated, fingering their way through the spongelike porosity of the rock. This highlights the nature of alpines; their habitat demands they forage for nutrition through lean matrixes. They have evolved in this environment. Plunking them in a richer medium does not make them unevolve. They like it this way. It also highlights how welcoming to plant roots this substance actually is.

Before beginning to drill, think about which plants you will be inserting. Some will grow a little faster than others; mats and trailers tend to bulk up faster than cushions. Decide if you want to use this piece to pamper difficult plants that may have been a challenge elsewhere. You might want to try growing alpines of varying difficulty levels. This will show you just what tufa does as a planting medium to enhance your chances of success. Silver or encrusted saxifrages are a great way to start. They are beautiful, a little miffy depending on variety, and with varying longevity from climate to climate, they might be perfect "lab plants." I strongly urge selecting the youngest, smallest specimens you can find—they establish better. I have lost my share of bigger beauties by not following this advice. Plant in early to mid-spring, before the weather heats up. Planted too late, the selection may not establish at all.

Once you have stacked the deck in your (and the plant's) favor, it is time to look at tufa. As mentioned, it is best to have stone that has been recently dug. "Young" tufa is softer and much easier to drill. Even young tufa can have hard spots, however; these generally look denser, smoother, and glassier than surrounding rock. Once you've tried to penetrate a couple of these spots you will begin to recognize them. You will need a fairly heavy-duty portable drill and a few good masonry drill bits in a couple of sizes. Always opt for quality; it will pay off.

Choose pieces of tufa that are largish—small ones will dry out too quickly. What does this mean? No smaller than a toaster, but bigger than a bread box is even better. Seat the piece in the trough; it usually looks best with the heavier, larger end downward. Play around with it. Better yet, play around with several pieces at the same time, inside the trough. Remember that you will be burying around thirty percent of the rock under the soil. You obviously will not be drilling there. To some extent, the way you place the piece of tufa in the container determines where the holes will go. Before starting to drill, take a careful, critical look at the entire stone. It will become obvious that too many holes in certain areas could compromise the strength of the piece. Guard against creating a perforation pattern along whose lines the tufa will break.

I fear the debate about how deep the hole ought to be may never be settled. There are those who steadfastly believe it should be not much more than an inch and a half deep, allowing the roots to do the penetrating. Others of the cognoscenti like to drill right through, so that the plant will be effectively rooting in the underlying medium. Personally, I don't see why anyone needs to land permanently in either camp. There are just too many variables. Each species is different, the same goes for climate (and microclimates). A tiny seedling inserted into a small, shallower hole is going to demand better babysitting, at least initially, than an alpine whose roots are launched into a deep chasm that communicates with the soil below.

I want to offer fair warning, too, about the angle of the drilled holes. If they are vertical, or perpendicular to the ground, they can accept rain, which helps with watering chores. If they are horizontal, or parallel to the ground, they will not receive rain. It might be a perfect spot for those rarities that resent wetness at the crown; in such a case, even a spot with an overhang could be used. It is a good idea to make sure the tufa is set deep enough into the ground that it will wick up moisture. If you create a dry habitat on purpose, though, remember that you are the keeper and tender of the plants in this xeric condition. Whatever angle the holes are, you will completely saturate the rock after planting, then continue to wet it down as needed until the plants get established.

Almost everyone working with genuine tufa agrees that placing organic matter such as compost, peat moss, or soil in the drilled hole is a big mistake. Since part of the extraordinary success with plants grown in tufa is being able to avoid pathogen-laden soil, I tend to agree with the "no organics at all" rule. Because of this, you will need to save every speck of tufa dust you drill out or that breaks off. This is incomparable backfill. It can be judiciously augmented with Turface, pumice, and smaller amounts of greensand and Spanish River Carbonatite. The last two contain welcome microminerals.

The actual planting into these tufa holes is a bit tricky. Try to come pretty close to bare-rooting your little plants. But please do them one at a time; baby plants left in the open air with exposed roots don't last long. Shake, tease, or even wash the soil off. The dry method can be kinder to the roots, wet ones tend to stretch and break, and wet roots are a bit harder to manipulate into the planting holes. Once most of the soil is off, hold the plant by leaf or stem and gently dangle the roots down into the hole using a chopstick or pencil to guide them, tucking in strays as you go. Begin to backfill by pouring the tufa dust in, using a folded index card or a small spoon. The crown of the little plant should end up just at the lip of the hole. I know, I have just described an operation that requires three hands. But gardeners are good at this

Tuck roots in, adding tufa dust.

sort of thing, aren't they? Tamp the mix in around the plant, gently using the eraser on a pencil. Water it in using a fine rosette. You may need to top it up after watering. Water in each plant at least a little as you proceed. Leaving a number of youngsters bare rooted and newly planted in dust is a recipe for failure. Once all plants are in, saturate the entire rock. Keep the whole thing out of the full baking sun for up to a week, and that's it.

I can offer a few suggestions of what, and what not, to grow directly in tufa. Don't waste precious tufa on plants you can grow anywhere—unless you intend to grow something lean and mean, and keep it tight, tiny, and in character, which could be a worthy exception. A few good choices include androsace, *Aquilegia jonesii*, asperula, campanula, douglasia, draba, edraianthus, certain eriogonums, alpine primula, saxifrage, and *Silene acaulis*. There are many others with which to experiment.

Sandwiching with Clay

This is a lesser-known technique for growing alpines in tufa rock. It involves using two (or more) slabs of stone, between which small plants can be placed and grown as part of an outcrop within a trough. It can actually be done dry or wet. The dry method is simply using potting soil and plants together to make a sandwich. The wet method is more elaborate. I first learned about it from the late Harvey Wrightman of Wrightman Alpines. Probably the trickiest part of this is obtaining the kind of tufa that can be split into what amounts to slices. Some batches seem to be easier than others. Freshly dug tufa is required and it definitely takes a skilled hand. Which is another way of saying I was not good at splitting it, even after watching carefully while it was done by an expert. Sometimes one can find a couple of slabs of tufa that are thin enough as is, but the split ones always fit together better because they are two halves of a common piece. Once the slices are ready, it is time to prepare the clay filling.

Slices of stone form this trough's tufa sandwich. Small plants thrive planted in the clay mixture between slabs. Clockwise from front center: *Androsace sempervivoides*, *Gypsophila aretioides* in crevice to left, *Primula* × *pubescens* 'Freedom', *Pterocephalus depressus*, *Primula allionii* 'Wharfedale Ling', and *Sempervivum* 'Gloriosum'.

Butter a slice of tufa with clay.

Position plant crowns at the edge.

Press slices together.

CLAY FILLING FOR SANDWICHED TUFA

Cedar Heights Goldart Airfloated Clay from Resco Products (I start with half a dishpan)
Spanish River Carbonatite or greensand (a generous handful)
water (added slowly)

Cedar Heights Goldart Airfloated Clay is a potter's clay that is used to glue the plants and slices together. It is prepared by mixing with a judicious amount of water and some minerals. The Wrightmans use Spanish River Carbonatite for mineral supplementation, but easier-to-find greensand also works. The mineral addition should equal no more than ten to fifteen percent of the mix.

1. BEFORE MIXING CLAY, SELECT SMALL, CHOICE, YOUNG ALPINES FOR THIS PROJECT.

2. STIR THE DRY CLAY PLUS A HANDFUL OF MINERALS TO-GETHER, THEN ADD WATER SLOWLY. Mix in until the whole is the consistency of a spreadable paste close to, but not quite as stiff as, peanut butter. The resultant clay should be sticky. It is difficult to offer an exact ratio of water; it is one of those things best done by feel, not to mention that the needed amount will vary by project.

3. SELECT AND PREPARE CHOICE BABY ALPINES. Shake and tease the soil out of the roots until they are close to soil free. A flat cement trowel is used to butter one slice of tufa with wet clay. Plants are placed onto this spread, with their crowns just at the edge of the stone. Then they are lightly pressed in.

4. SANDWICH THE PLANTS AND CLAY TOGETHER WITH THE OTHER SLICE OF TUFA—LIKE A DOUBLE-DECKER CLUB SANDWICH. This can be continued for however many decks you want your tufa sandwich to have. During a workshop, I watched as people combined five, six, even seven slices of rock.

The sandwiches can be made free standing and added to a trough later, or they can be pressed together in situ in the trough, slab by slab. Part of the trick, both aesthetically and culturally, is to keep the crevice holding the plants as narrow as possible. These impressive chunky sandwiches can be placed upright, perpendicular to the ground facing the sky, or they can be tilted at a more oblique angle. A couple things I absolutely adore about this technique is that no two pieces ever look remotely alike, and it is wholly absorbing as you are in the throes of creation. I don't care how sophisticated you are, this will throw you back into the state of mind you had during your most engrossing childhood project. It did just that to a fleet of experienced rock gardeners at a workshop I attended.

Time will fly by until you look up and the sun is westering, airfloated clay is smeared across your nose, and you are gazing upon an enchanting piece to set into your garden. You will be amazed at what you just created. Stepping back from my first one, I certainly was.

Double-decker sandwiched tufa.

A few seasons after making that first tufa sandwich, I can report additional items of note. The sandwiches I made are holding up fairly well, especially those crevices that were kept narrow. The mix of clay, because it is never fired, never quite hardens. This can and has led to some erosion. Some of this can be averted by pressing chips or flakes of tufa or stone directly into any gaps. Also, where plants have grown away well and filled their cavities, there is less washing out, thanks to the stabilizing roots and the little domes of plants that shed rain. At the end of the first winter, I had lost only one plant. It was my fault. I had coveted a cushion too large for this process, had not bare rooted it enough, and needed to settle it in a wider crevice (even though I had squashed it pretty flat). All in all, not a failure of the process, rather a direct result of hubris. I knew better, didn't I? Apparently not.

It is true that sandwiches can come apart. A rapid and deep, freezing plunge in temperature can in effect explode the slices apart. I believe the trouble begins when you start to think of the clay as mortar holding it all together. The clay is only a binder, in that it holds better than plain soil. It is not Gorilla Glue. The sandwiches must be

Cushions in a sandwich.

constructed soundly. It helps to wedge the sandwich rather tightly into its container. This can be helped by bracing it with chinks of smaller stones. I anticipate that any attempt to replace a plant would be exasperating at best. Which is why I believe in overplanting these crevices. Better to solve an embarrassment of riches than a dearth. And there are nooks at the base of the sandwiches just begging for more plants. Add something unexpected: a daphne or salix to mimic those woody plants twisting out of rock crevices at altitude. Place a penstemon in the corner, the dome of a dianthus, the curtain of a trailer. Ultimately these may just become your favorite troughs, and the stone construction is the star player.

PLANTS APPROPRIATE *for* TROUGHS

THIS CHAPTER WILL OFFER descriptions of plants suitable for use inside a hypertufa trough. They are broken down into anchor plants, ground covers, buns and cushions, droolers, succulents, and shade plants. There is a miscellaneous last section for those that resist categorizing. This is not a comprehensive list by any means. I have tried to walk a line regarding the difficulty level of the plants, choosing to make the lion's share relatively growable for most situations. There is no section for sun plants (as there is for shade choices) simply because most mountain plants are sun lovers. Unless otherwise noted, the subject will require full sun.

ANCHOR PLANTS

A relatively vertical plant in a trough usually forms the focal point. I say "usually" because stones can also be used as an anchor, though not in the same way as a plant. The anchor plant frequently is a small shrub or a dwarf tree. It might be upright or rounded, pillar shaped or windswept and contorted. Consider using a delicately leafed deciduous willow with all the Japanese panache of ikebana, or a glossy broadleaf or weeping hemlock for semi-shade. The growth speed of conifers is important, because you don't want your specimen to outgrow its space too quickly, although the contained shrub often exhibits a tendency to slower growth than one in the ground. Look for species that put on an inch of growth or less per year.

Gentiana acaulis, happy in a sunny trough.

107

When I am working on a miniature landscape, I tend to fall into one or two modi operandi. Sometimes I have an idea of a look I want in a shrub and go hunting to find one that fits my idea. Other times, I fall under the enchantment of the character of a shrub first and, with that woody plant in hand, get inspired to fill out the rest of the design using it as a starting point.

Conifers

Chamaecyparis selections provide verdant textures that are rich and lovely in a trough. Most have a mounded profile. Two beautiful named forms are *C. obtusa* 'Hage' and *C. obtusa* 'Ellie B'. Outside the mounding category and more upright are *C. obtusa* 'Spiralis' and *C. obtusa* 'Thoweil'.

Juniperus communis 'Compressa' is constantly in demand—the exclamation point people seem to be looking for. Narrow and vertical, this juniper or even a collection of them are easy to use in the design process; just don't place one precisely in the middle like the candle on a one-year-old's cupcake. The anchor is always best placed asymmetrically. A very shrub-centric design could be made using a charming little clutch of these junipers, a grove of exclamation points. *Juniperus chinensis* 'Shimpaku' is slow and easily pruned into a windswept look.

For an upright conifer with a more conical shape and a sturdy winter constitution, use *Picea glauca* 'Jean's Dilly' or 'Pixie'. These have cone-shaped, Christmas tree–like habits with dense, fine-textured needles. They will handle protracted cold as well as strong winter sun and most exposures you throw at them, except for dense shade.

There is an uncanny 'rightness' about the balance of a cone and a sphere together. I remember looking at old images of the 1939 World's Fair in New York. The trademark of the entire event happened to be two structures in these same shapes, called the Trylon and the Perisphere. The designers of those icons had discovered what gardeners have long known. There is a nifty balance, pairing an upright conifer with a rounded one. If the taller plant in the trough looks too spare, try adding a mounded chamaecyparis planted near its base, anchoring the anchor plant.

Picea glauca contains many interesting dwarf cultivars: 'Blue planet', 'Elf', 'Hobbit', and 'Humpty Dumpty', for example. I would not want to be without *P. abies* 'Pusch'. With purple-red cones in spring, it is worth seeking out.

Pinus offers another group for full sun. The smallest of the mugo pines are tough and adaptable. Search out true miniatures like *P. mugo* 'Donna's Mini' and *P. mugo*

A collection of dwarf conifers ready for planting.

Ball and cone shapes.

'Michelle'. Two other pines that are handsome and a bit different are *P. leucodermis* 'Schmidtii' and *P. parviflora* 'Kinpo'. These both have a strong presence and are reliable and well structured.

To keep almost any pine tidy and tight, learn to candle the new growth. New growth resembles a candle, hence the term for trimming it. In spring, once the growing tips have extended, pinch them back. Do not remove the candle entirely. You want a little new growth yearly on these plants; they seem to resent complete removal. Pines will not break from old wood. This means that if they are cut back into the branch or trunk, they will not produce new growth to cover that, you will be left with an unsightly stump. Pinch back the candles by one third, or up to two-thirds their length. Use your fingers, not a tool, as a blade cut will invariably result in odd-looking growth later on. The blade will shear through the immature whorl

Picea abies 'Pusch'.

of needles on a single plane; a finger pinch results in a natural look. For a congested, rounded cushion, candle all the growing tips, or selectively candle certain ones to create asymmetry.

Tsuga canadensis is perfect for a semi-shady spot. Good dwarf hemlocks to look for are *T. canadensis* 'Abbots Pygmy' and *T. canadensis* 'Minuta'. *Tsuga canadensis* 'Cole's Prostrate' offers a weeping habit. Unique among the others because of its beautiful layered structure is *T. diversifolia* 'Loowit'.

There are a fair number of excellent rock gardeners out there who believe that conifers do not belong among alpines, period. And there is no doubt whatsoever that beautiful troughs can be planted without them. One thorny issue is that these woody plants simply outgrow their space (and thus their welcome) over time. Each trough gardener must find a comfort zone with the problem. No matter how dwarf

Pinus and *Picea* selections on display.

or slow, these shrubs do continue inexorably to grow. Be extremely vigilant in your selections. A "dwarf" picea is still honorably and rightly considered dwarf if it matures at five or six feet—after all, the species itself in the forest might reach up to eighty feet tall. Baby conifers can be devilishly adorable, so arm yourself with a little buyer's resistance, read the labels, and look up the cultivars carefully. What you seek is a yearly growth rate of an inch or less. But with this tinier growth rate, the price will usually climb surprisingly high, albeit quite logically. A baby that spends only a year in a pot before being saleable is relatively cheap to produce. One that a grower must watch over and tend for five, six, or seven years before it is ready for market is not.

Other woody plants

Though by no means easy to keep, I'd be remiss if I didn't mention the dwarf daphnes. They are a pretty inspirational genus, with long bloom times and beautifully scented flowers, a compact shape and small shining leaves. *Daphne × mantensiana* is gorgeous and highly scented, with light purple flowers opening from darker buds. If it's your shrub of choice, though, understand it will need some solid winter protection. *Daphne retusa* appears to be a good deal sturdier. It has white blooms opening from dark purple buds and dark green glossy leaves. *Daphne* 'Lawrence Crocker' is one to covet and search out. It remains small and bears lavender-pink flowers. It was discovered in Oregon by its namesake, one of the founders of Siskiyou Rare Plant Nursery. This plant would be the star of any trough. *Daphne petraea* is another choice and very slow-growing beauty. There are many more daphnes to discover—both species and cultivars. The treasure hunt is part of the fun.

Be forewarned, however: daphnes will also break your heart. The sudden, dreaded daphne death can spirit away your specimen without warning. Once decline sets in, it is next to impossible to stop; no one seems to be able to point to a definitive cause. Some say they are sensitive to bacterial or fungal disorders and absolutely perfect drainage is essential. Proper light and air are important, but never cook a daphne on a southern slope. It needs to be grown on the dry side. Keep the base of the plant free of litter that can harbor disease. If you are willing to go the extra step and form a tufa crevice inside a trough, you might try cultivars of *Daphne arbuscula* and *D.* × *hendersonii*. The joys to be had from this diverse flowering clan are many, and each gardener must test the waters, see what thrives in any given microclimate. The trials and even the tribulations are worth it.

Enkianthus perulatus 'Compactus', though difficult to find, is an absolute jewel. It will take in the neighborhood of 50 years to get past knee height, so slow-growing barely describes it. Because of this and its relative rarity, its cost can be high. 'Compactus' requires acid soil. While it is rounded as a youngster, with age the top flattens out with beautiful branch structure and typical enkianthus leaves. Flowers are borne in spring, covering the plant with waxy, white, downward-facing bells. It is a showstopper in fall when the foliage turns an almost indescribable flame-orange.

Leiophyllum buxifolium 'Prostratum' is worth every effort to find and keep. Like *Enkianthus perulatus* 'Compactus', it wants acidic conditions. Well-draining sandy soil is appreciated, but it will not tolerate drought or heat or baking sun. There is nothing quite like this plant mounding up and over the side of a trough. Its tiny, shiny leaves are light reflective. Buds are pink, opening to small white flowers with fluffy stamens. The charm of 'Prostratum' is hard to nail down in words. Seeing one in bud equals wanting one.

The genus *Salix* offers another group of plants with which to experiment. A few, *Salix* × *boydii* in particular, are known to be difficult. This is an exquisite gem, with felted dark battleship-gray leaves and a perfect little tree habit. Deep soil, natural tufa rock near the roots, and good winter snow cover all seem to help keep it happy—or

Daphne 'Lawrence Crocker'.

Daphne × *hendersonii* (ex Rick Lupp).

those things at least offer a chance for you to keep this finnicky plant at all. I know of one that has been doing okay for about four years now, but the relatively gigantic trough it is in may be part of the reason. The trough is a tremendous bowl several feet deep and about four feet across. Large chunks of natural tufa are sunk deeply nearby. Not coincidentally, this is a place that choice silver saxifrages agree to inhabit as well. It is the first place I will put a rare treasure hoping for longevity.

Then there are other willows, *Salix yezoalpina* for example, that display thuggish behavior, greedily gobbling up all available root room inside a trough, even sending roots downward through the drainage hole questing for more room. Even so, I have a soft spot for this bruiser, with its gnarled roots and branches and its stunning display early in spring, when the silky silver leaves begin to unfurl. I choose to wrestle with it as a single specimen, in a tall, large cylinder trough. If it is placed anywhere near soil (including the stone dust cracks in a terrace), give it a quarter turn a few times a year, or the roots will penetrate the drainage hole and dive down.

Salix arctica var. *petraea* is a quintessential deciduous weeping shrub. This one is procurable as well as possible to grow, and will stay in scale. As a youngster, it requires some pruning and shaping, but hardly any may be needed after half a dozen years or so. When leaves first emerge in spring, and as the branches weep over the side of the container, it offers the ravishing impression of a Japanese painting.

Salix arctica var.
petraea.

Other ideas for anchor plants

The smaller the trough, the more miniature a vertical accent should be. An alternative to the traditional little tree might be one of the shrubby penstemons, like *Penstemon rupicola*. *Moltkia petraea* is a slow-growing, shrubby plant with striking blue flowers, forming a mound of open branchwork tipped with blooms. Once established in a trough, this plant can be long lived. It is even possible to skip the shrubby material and still have a vertical accent. A small grass or sedge can stand in, or the swords of dwarf iris leaves. These last two will pull the eye upward, and either one looks utterly charming in the lee of a handsome stone. Never place a five- or six-inch iris with a dwarf shrub, however—each will throw the other out of scale, especially when the iris is in flower.

Iris as an anchor plant. Here, *Iris* 'Jive' and 'Heart Stopper' are combined with *Calluna vulgaris* 'Orange Queen'.

The more you garden in troughs, the more you will find that once the shrub and stones are in place, the bones of your design are, too. The rest, as they say, is icing on the cake. So now we get to the icing.

TINY GROUND COVERS

When choosing minute ground covers, select for leaf size first. Smaller is better. The final height of the plants must work with your other plants. A two-inch mat is too tall if your miniature tree is only six inches. This goes for the height of the flower stems as well, although most of us will soften our rules in the face of an adorable patch of trembling spring flowers. Nothing helps along the believability of a miniature landscape like a convincing ground cover, perfectly in scale. Think of how an expanse of turf performs in a full-sized garden. But the lawn does not also offer us blooms, and many tiny ground covers for troughs can give us that, too.

The ultimate "lawn" for a trough just might be moss. There is a glow that moss gives off when it goes into growth. It radiates vitality. We can, of course, simply be patient, place our troughs in an area that already has moss, and wait for the moss to colonize the container. People often try to find ways to import mosses, but think twice about this. Never strip them out of the woodlands, and always ask permission on private property. Most people treasure the moss on their land, just as you would. There are specific cultural requirements when moving a moss, and they are not that easy to grow. Some dos and don'ts: don't move a moss from a sunny spot to a shady site, or the other way around. Mosses also have a preferred orientation. Transplanting will not be successful if a moss is taken from a vertical location and placed in a horizontal one. Success is usually much more assured by simply picking up a rock or piece of wood that has moss growing on it already and placing that in your trough. Make conditions as moss friendly as you can. Most mosses want a low pH. They like moisture and do not thrive in competition with other plants, including weeds. From there on, it will be up to the whims of the mosses to release the spores to grow and prosper.

Antennaria selections form a perennial silver rug. One favorite is *Antennaria dioica* 'Nyewoods Variety', with ballet-pink blooms and a bright silver edge to each sage-green leaf. For thick, dense silver coverage fairly quickly, choose A. *parviflora* 'McClintock'. They all divide readily and recover from it well. *Antennaria aromatica* has almost-white foliage that is so extremely congested it gets mistaken for a choice

Impermanent Plants

Raoulia australis in a free-form trough with *Orostachys spinosa.*

There are a number of not-quite-hardy ground covers that are worth mentioning. These may have a tag on them boasting zone 6 or even lower, but I suspect they need to be in zone 7b or warmer. They are worth considering for your trough, though, especially if they offer long-blooming flowers or distinctive texture. *Laurentia fluviatilis* (both the blue and the white form) is low, dense, and floriferous, offering blossoming for most of the season. A two-inch pot of it will enlarge respectably in one season to four or five times the original size, enough to make a real impact. *Lindernia grandiflora* drapes over edges in a short time and continues to throw its vibrant blue-purple blossoms for most of the season. *Leptinella squalida* 'Platt's Black' is made up of dense, tiny fronds that are fernlike. The more sun you give it, the darker bronze it will be. *Mazus radicans* gives us an atypical leaf. Olive-green with darker spots and stipples, the best description of the effect is reptilian. Blossoms are little cream snapdragons touched in the throat with yellow and violet. *Muehlenbeckia axillaris* 'Nana' is the tiniest of the wire vines, forming a patch of minute, olive-colored leaves on thread-thin black stems. And if silver makes you swoon, you will be helpless before the tribe of *Raoulia.* There are a number of them, the names are sometimes mixed up; look for *R. australis.* They enchant by spreading their delicate silver skin across your trough and are hard to resist. They can succumb to summer humidity as well as winter wet, so never seem to be permanent.

Winter moisture has a lot to do with these plants being impermanent, so too does their bent for flowering all summer and not having the "juice" to get through the winter.

Globularia repens
growing directly in tufa.

Eriogonum, and is just as slow growing. There is a caterpillar that sometimes shows up on pussytoes. If the plant is small and choice, they can do some damage. If you see white webbing, they are present, and because the plants are so light in color, this can be hard to catch.

I originally received *Erigeron scopulinus* from the late Norman Singer, and think fondly of him when I tuck some into a trough. It is a very flat grower with tiny leaves not typical of the genus. The flowers are perfect little white daisies with a gold eye, always in scale. You can see it in a rock garden on page 82.

Eunomia oppositifolia is sometimes still found under the genus *Aethionema*. Its rounded gray-green leaves sport fragrant, lilac-pink flowers very early in spring.

Globularia cordifolia subsp. *nana* and its even tinier sibling, *Globularia repens*, have blackish foliage in winter. This shows up wonderfully against lighter-colored

Pterocephalus depressus.

gravel or stone. The flowers of both are small balls of steel blue, but rarely arrive in abundance. When they do, though, it is a showstopper, especially when planted in a hole drilled in tufa.

Penstemon davidsonii var. *menziesii* 'Microphyllus' is a mat former with tiny leaves about the size of a lentil. One of the smallest in the genus, this cultivar has beautiful blue to violet spring flowers that look startlingly large for the size of the plant. Unfortunately, it does not look its best in a nursery pot. Once planted in a roomier trough, though, it begins to spread its toes into the soil and thrive. Don't fry this in afternoon sun.

Pterocephalus depressus has flowers that resemble scabious. A relatively new introduction from Morocco, it is a hardy selection. Appealing, crinkled gray-green leaves form mats, and sitting directly on top of the mats appear dark wine-red buds that open pink and eventually form pink to silvery seed heads.

Sedums can fulfill the ground cover role too. But because many can grow quickly, do not place them too close to tiny, choice, slow-growing treasures that may be swamped. For blue-green to lilac and rose tones, try *Sedum hispanicum* var. *minus*. The best colors will show up only if plants are given lots of sun and heat. For deep cranberry winter color, include *Sedum album* 'Coral Carpet'. The inclination of sedums is to colonize. They will root down wherever a piece of the plant falls. For shade, the native *Sedum nevii* is the answer. It consists of little apple-green rosettes and slowly forms a patch. Sheer off flower buds to keep it tight.

Thymes should be mentioned in this category. Many are thugs both above ground and below, overwhelming a planting on top and filling up the root room

Sedum hispanicum var. *minus.*

beneath. Opt for only the smallest, most refined ones. Try *Thymus serpyllum* 'Elfin', *T. serpyllum* 'Minus' and *T. praecox* 'Highland Cream'. The sage-green and cream variegation of 'Highland Cream' is elegant, and the plant is very slow growing.

The veronicas offer many candidates. *Veronica rupestris* forms pools of purple-blue blossoms. Try the golden-leaved *V. repens* 'Sunshine' for contrast. From Turkey comes *V. bombycina*, with the most densely felted, white leaf imaginable, and deep blue blooms. This can be difficult to keep. Two others that can prove challenging are *V. caespitosa* and *V. thymoides* subsp. *pseudocinerea*, both lovely but resenting humidity. Then there is *V. oltensis*, easy to grow and probably the tiniest-leaved of the genus, creating an elegant lace doily spangled with blooms.

Veronica bombycina
subsp. *froediniana*.

Beyond beauty, ground covers are useful for erosion control. If your design features level changes, especially steep ones, it can be a challenge to keep those levels defined and sound. A patch of ground cover in a trough can be used to hold the soil and gravel in place. Given a little time, the plant roots will knit things together, providing durability on a slope.

BUNS AND CUSHIONS

Probably the most classic alpine shape is the cushion. I don't know a rock gardener alive who isn't inspired by these plants. Nothing is so breathtaking above timberline than to come upon the rock-hard congested dome of a cushion. No matter if it is out of flower, it is easier to see the geometry that way. Perhaps it is a perfect hemisphere of a draba, or even a rare androsace. Though perfect geometry is stunning, sometimes the circle is not perfect. In its own way, this is as or more enchanting than the unblemished dome. What has usually altered the inexorable roundness is a rock or ledge close against the plant. It may have turned into a pillowy crescent shape around the stone. This, by the way, can take time and patience to reproduce in a trough. Another common sight in nature is more than one specimen of the species in a clutch together. This is achievable in your trough at home. But copy nature.

At elevation, the individuals in a colony of domes are rarely if ever the same age. There will be the large mothership a bit upslope from most of the other plants, because self-sowing generally progresses downhill. The largest dome may be the size of a half softball, then there may be a few half golf balls, then a few half marble–sized hemispheres. You may even notice the tiny tufts of newborns. I have seen seedlings of drabas the size of a split pea bearing a bright yellow flower or two trembling on thin stems. On rare occasions, you even may find a couple different cushion plant species cohabitating in the same general area. If you do, consider yourself charmed. People who climb entire mountains to seek out alpines in their habitat will tell you that you have stumbled upon a natural bunnery.

It could prove worthwhile to document this find with photos and footnotes, poking fingers into the scree, identifying rocks, the substrate, and so on. Most people, though, come to a silent standstill, just basking in the bunnery. As it should be.

Among the ranks of the buns and cushions are plenty of rare, difficult subjects to try. I believe in approaching this list in a more relaxed and broader sense. If the plant in question is a pleasant hemisphere and plays well with others in captivity, include it! The phrase "in character" is bandied about in rock garden circles. This is when the plant looks as though it is growing on its preferred mountaintop, even though in reality it may be in a trough on someone's deck. To achieve this character, give the plants as much sun as they want, not as much as you can spare after the pool, vegetable garden, and roses have taken their cut. Alpines won't negotiate. Offer perfect drainage and lean soil. Employ the trick of protecting cushions from the moist ground with thin stone flakes carefully puzzle-pieced under the skirts around the crown.

Cushion plants to try

Androsace carnea and *A.* 'Millstream' are growable. The beautiful *A. sarmentosa* and *A. sempervivoides* are also growable, but are not really cushion shaped. The former can outgrow its space. *Androsace ciliata* and *A. mucronifolia* can be kept for a while, at least. When you attempt *A. helvetica* or *A. vandellii*, you have moved onto difficult ground, to be sure.

Arabis androsacea is the one arabis that fulfills the shape. It creates a slightly fuzzy dome with white flowers and is rather underused by rock gardeners.

Asperula pontica and *A. gussonii* fall into a medium range of difficulty. *Asperula suberosa* and *A. sintenisii* seem more moisture sensitive, tending to melt down in high humidity.

The Bunnery

Nature in her wisdom led these cushion species to take a very strong and protective shape. The hemisphere allows the sometimes-merciless wind to flow over the plant in a very aerodynamic way. It is a shape that is much less easily damaged when the inevitable shower of gravel and rocks rattles down from above.

Buns offer an additional defense against those bouncing stones—they have cores made up of durable stuffing. It works this way: unlike taller perennials, cushions hold on to their old foliage. This stuffing performs multiple functions—it makes the plant more resilient and it provides insulation. Interestingly, this interior packing is one cause of failure for those trying to grow alpines at sea level. Buns can absorb humidity like a sponge, leading to rot, browning, and finally the collapse of the plant.

Ultimately, given the short growing season on mountaintops, it is economical for the plant to put forth new growth just at the tips of last year's growth. Slowly, the size of the dome increases in this way. It also allows the alpine bun to skip that step herbaceous perennials must always make— erupting anew from the ground every year, producing stalks, leaves, flowers, and fruit all in one season. That would take up time the cushion plant does not have, since it must flower and set seed before the shockingly early onset of winter. The alpine habitat has taught its plants to push out flower buds often when icy meltwater is still running over the plants' toes. Alpines can begin to grow and their roots can take up nutrients at just a little above freezing. Their adaptations include flowering big, early, and low on the cushion.

These are traits that humans admire. Some species even set flower buds the fall before. This makes it possible for rapid early bloom, allowing whatever precious warmth there may be in the short mountain summer to be dedicated to setting and ripening seed, a process that requires more heat than flowering does. The season is so short that first snow can fly again as early as August.

Armeria juniperifolia grows into a perfect half baseball. Forms exist in white and every gradation of pink. Because they are easy, and rock gardeners like challenges, they are rarely included in cushion lists. I am a fan.

Many *Dianthus* species are beauties, but most are too large. *Dianthus microlepis* is probably the most choice and small. *Dianthus freynii, D. gratianopolitanus* 'Petite', and *D. alpinus* are only three among many others to explore in this prolific genus.

Draba rigida is a favorite, so flat to the ground that it looks like a pat of moss with delicate, tiny flowers on thin stems. *Draba dedeana* is a white-flowered bun, but is not

Dianthis gratianopolitanus 'Petite'.

easy to find true to name. Others to hunt for are *D. densifolia* and *D. ventosa*. *Draba oligosperma* is harder to find and keep. For a challenge, or to be grown in an alpine house: *D. polytricha*, *D. mollissima*, and *D. cappadocica*. These last three are gorgeous queens of the species; they can (with luck) be grown outside for a year or two, perhaps, under optimal conditions.

    Eriogonum ovalifolium and its varieties are choice. There are other species, too—some too large for a trough and some not cushion shaped. All have great character but want xeric conditions. The silver-felted foliage is beautiful, but it is tough to get them to flower well in the Northeast. *Eriogonum kennedyi* is flat and congested. The foliage is silver gray, the flowers white, sometimes with a stain of pink. *Eriogonum caespitosum* subsp. *douglasii* is another choice but challenging species. All eriogonums are deep rooted, so they will need some depth to grow well.

Eriogonum ovalifolium.

Petrocallis pyreniaca.

Gypsophila aretioides is not grown for its flowers. Four or five pink specks on a mature cushion are the most I have ever seen. The foliage is hard as a rock and it will picturesquely morph around stones.

Petrocallis pyreniaca is affectionately known as the pink draba. This is a European cushion with grayish leaves; the flowers are pink to lilac, rarely white, and are vanilla scented.

A race of sun-lovers from the American West, plants in the genus *Phlox* are for the most part too spreading in their habit to include in a trough. However, there are three microphloxes that are charming and well behaved, tight, and slow growing, with tiny leaves and proportionately tiny flowers. *Phlox subulata* 'Herbert' and 'Betty' have blooms that are pink and lilac respectively; they were selected by the late Dick Redfield and named in honor of his siblings. *Phlox subulata* 'Sileniflora' has pale pink buds that open to white flowers; it is a selection by the celebrated plantsman H. Lincoln Foster. In a large trough, consider using *P. kelseyi* in one of its forms, such as 'Lemhi Purple' or 'Lemhi Midnight', which both bear dark, rich purple flowers. More challenging are two subspecies of *P. caespitosa*: *pulvinata* and *condensata*. The former has blooms from white to pink; the latter is smaller and always bears white flowers.

Not usually included as cushion plants, a few primulas can legitimately be allowed in. When I first tried varieties of *Primula allionii*, I remember the losses and the

Phlox subulata 'Betty' and *Phlox kelseyi*.

frustration that came with them. Attempting a few types much later on with success, I wondered for an instant, had I become that much better as a grower? Since then, I learned that the *P. allionii* selections I succeed with are hybrids, not the species; they usually include some *P. marginata* in their bloodlines. *Primula allionii* 'Wharfedale Ling' is growable in a trough, especially with tufa rock near the roots or with the addition of pumice to the soil. It has a white center and a purple-pink rim on the blooms; the foliage huddles up into a nice mound. Its cousin, *P. allionii* 'Hemswell Blush' has purple blossoms and a yellow center, and is a bit larger in both leaf and flower. The climate you garden in will have a profound effect on your success with these. They will not like hot and dry, but neither will they like sticky and soggy. Those in cool, temperate environments will have a much longer primrose vocabulary.

The name *Saxifraga* literally means stone-breaker, and this genus does love to grow in crevices of stone. Saxes seem to resent organic matter in their soil. They are finicky in general, so if you have struggled with them, ditch the peat and opt for a purely mineral soil. (Easier said than done, of course.) Or, try planting saxes directly into tufa rock and incorporate the tufa into your trough design. There many members of this desirable clan that fit the cushion plant category.

The encrusted saxifrages are a little more amenable to cultivation than the Kabschias. But just a little, so don't relax too much. They are like silver sea urchins adpressed to an underwater jetty. They dome up, or spread elegantly through an elongated crevice. Individual rosettes are worthy of the up-close examination of a jeweler. The silver effect comes from tiny pits of lime deposits on the leaves. Dot patterns differ, but most have exquisite lines along the leaf edges. All *Saxifraga paniculata* selections are worth growing, they vary in leaf shape, size and texture; some are rounded, some pointed. A few, *S. cuneifolia* and *S.* 'Winifred Bevington' among them, are greener overall. *Saxifraga andrewsii* is bigger, with sword-shaped, toothed leaves.

The hybrids using *Saxifraga longifolia* are interesting. The straight species is monocarpic: once it blooms, the plant dies. The hybrids can waiver back and forth on this behavior (all flowering rosettes will die, but not always the whole plant) so it behooves the gardener to have a few pups of their favorites rooting somewhere in the wings. The chance of losing a large, mature specimen is great once all the flowering stems begin to elongate.

Saxifraga 'Southside Seedling' is believed to be one of these hybrids. In flower, everybody wants this one. Inflorescences rise more than a foot high, the branched stalks profusely spangled with white blooms heavily blotched with red near the base of each petal. *Saxifraga* 'Tumbling Waters' has an even longer flower stalk, putting on an extraordinary floral show with arching panicles of white flowers. Both forms offer high drama, though it usually exhausts the plant. I love these best when they are not in flower. The individual rosettes are large and sculptural. Therefore, when a flower scape is forming, it saddens me to know the big starburst will be gone.

Naturally, everybody wants the tiniest, slowest-growing "silver" in the biggest specimen that can be bought. It is rare to find the smallest species grown large for sale for very good reasons. It takes plenty of time, often years, and watchful care to bring it to maturity. Growers will face just what you will in trying to get them there. For what it's worth, here are a few of the tiny, finely crafted encrusted saxes: *Saxifraga valdensis*, *S. cochlearis* 'Minor' and *S. paniculata* var. *minutifolia*. In the trade, these have sometimes gotten muddled together.

I want to offer my best insight, gathered over the years trying different strategies growing these gems. Plant saxifrages early in the season before the air and everything else heats up. (This advice applies to all alpines, actually, which benefit from being planted earlier than later.) We all know that the cool of early spring is very different than the sticky heat that comes at the end of spring. In less-than-sun-drenched areas like the Northeast, offer them more sun than shade. Be cautious about tipping too far into the sun, however; it can lead to crispy plants. But too much shade, especially with humidity, can promote rot. It is a fine line, and I often move the container once or twice in the same season. The last tip is to sandwich the roots between pieces of real tufa. This substance can be the magic bullet for many difficult alpines; it works and is worth the effort to track it down if you can.

Silene acaulis is a tight, mossy mountain plant with small, delicate pink flowers. As far as growing difficulty goes, consider it in the middle range. Do not let it dry out or cook, but do offer enough sun for it to thrive. Selected forms include *S. acaulis* 'Heidi', which is lovely and vigorous.

Vitaliana primuliflora (moved by some authorities into the genus *Androsace*) is an early-flowering, choice, silvery leaved plant with lemon-colored flowers. It is grow-able and worthwhile.

Cushionhood is in the eye of the beholder. Experienced alpine cognoscenti may only consider the rarest, tightest, most congested, and difficult plants to be legiti-mate cushions. I throw my net wider than that. I see no reason why even some suc-culents should not be included. The tighter-growing, more-generously pupped hens and chicks will cushion up nicely. Sempervivums come from above timberline and are authentic alpines. And I defy any cushion expert to sneer at a well-grown *Sem-pervivum arachnoideum* in its webbed and silvery prime.

For success, a lot will depend on the gardener's bunsmanship, to coin a word. By this, I mean the skill the grower uses to mimic the natural home of the plant, plus any and all heroic (even ridiculous) measures to get the cushion to be a cushion and not splay open, stretch, or go bald in the center. One trick that may repair a bald spot is to sift clean, sharp sand into it. The idea is to get a gritty medium near the stem bases, so they may root and push new growth. *Dianthus* will sometimes respond to this. Grow your plants lean, don't overfeed or overwater. Give them as vast an amount of sunshine as they crave and as is possible in your locality. Cheat a little. Discrete grooming and pruning can help. A plant that may grow looser on the flat just may pillow up when tucked between two stones in a rock crevice. When you find buns and cushions on a mountain under a brilliant, windswept sky, they are usually growing tight and congested. In a trough, by whatever method—be it scientific, cosmetic, honorable, or sneaky—we try to get as close to this ideal as possible.

Saxifraga 'Southside Seedling' starting to bloom.

DROOLERS

This is an affectionate term for cascading plants. Nothing softens the hard geometry of a trough like a growing thing tumbling joyfully over the edge, giving the impression that the plants and container have been there forever and lending an atmosphere of antiquity to everything nearby. There are actually several ways that plants drool over edges. Those trailing styles will define how they are used.

The overly zealous

This includes the most exuberant plants, those that extend themselves in a tangle of blossoming stems, having the effect of a waterfall. Many in this group are bigger than is practical in a trough.

Androsace lanuginosa is a lovely octopus. Its awkwardly long shoots end in rosettes, which produce umbels of primrose-like flowers sometime in June. As a plant, it is unwieldy at both ends of its season. At both times, the gardener must decide whether to trim the tangle back, each cut sacrificing a rosette and thus some flowers.

Artemisia lagopus is a winner if you want the turbulence of silver cumulous clouds pouring over the side of your trough. There is not a lot of information out there on this wormwood. It seems to be rare in the trade.

Chaenorhinum origanifolium is a chimera. In full flower, it looks blowsy. But tighter early growth makes it seem to fit into the cushion plant category. Cut it back after the inevitable post-flowering dishevelment and it will tighten up again—unless you want it to seed around, which it will do. Enthusiastically.

Lonicera crassifolia is amenable to shade or sun. This adorable honeysuckle does not seem like a beast the first year or so, although it can travel a yard in every direction in the rock garden and root as it goes. It has shiny, thick, round leaves and if you keep the stems trimmed, it will cluster nicely. Buds are pink and flowers open butter yellow, then deepen in color as they age. The leaves turn a rich burgundy in colder weather.

Origanum 'Kent Beauty' has such an incredibly long bloom time that annual gardeners will sometimes choose it for window boxes. When it comes to oreganos, I have very little resistance. I like to grow this big beauty by itself in a trough, preferably raised up to enjoy the drama. Many bigger droolers are rewarding in monoculture. (That is, grown alone in a good-sized trough.) The ornamental "hops" it produces are actually rose-stained bracts. The flowers themselves are tucked inside these and

Lonicera crassifolia.

are tiny and more fleeting. When the hops eventually fade to light brown, the stems can be cut back and new foliage will appear, as will, often, a second show of flowers. Also look for *O.* 'Amethyst Falls'.

Droolers that stay in scale

Gypsophila franzii 'Nana Compacta' cascades six to eight inches over the side and bears tiny pale pink flowers.

Herniaria glabra 'Sea Foam' features subtle cream and green variegation and floats out and over the trough edges. In the heat of summer, variegation vanishes, but will return when nights cool off.

Saponaria 'Bressingham' in the front pocket, with *Silene uniflora* 'Druett's Variegated'. In back: *Abies koreana* 'Kohout's Ice Breaker' with *Delosperma* 'Jewel of Desert Opal', *Erigeron leiomerus*, and a baby *Salvia daghestanica*.

Saponaria 'Bressingham' is the most compact soapwort I know of. Bright carmine flowers keep coming for a long while.

Silene uniflora 'Compacta' is a catchfly with charm and staying power. Its foliage is blue-green. Buds are pink, opening pure white, exhibiting the classic inflated calyx below the flower found in many silenes. This will drape over the side substantially, and throw self-sown seedlings. After flowering, it is up to the gardener to deadhead (in which case more flowers will usually ensue) or to sit back and enjoy the balloon-like pods while the seed ripens.

Do trees and shrubs drool? Well, we know they weep, and it amounts to the same thing, at least with miniatures in a container. A woody plant that cascades over a trough edge is an aesthetic coup that adds character. *Tsuga canadensis* 'Cole's Prostrate' is a well-known weeper, sometimes grafted to start weeping at a taller point. *Salix repens* and its various forms can trail substantially. But the quintessential woody weeper has to be *Salix arctica* var. *petraea*. This gets gorgeously gnarled over time and will throw its limbs out and over an edge, looking like a tortured shrub clinging to a rock on the side of a mountain in Japan. It takes time to establish, preferring to be root-bound, so don't overpot it.

The dynamic of cascading can sometimes use a little help along the way. Always place the intended drooler at the trough edge facing the source of light. Light will encourage the plant to reach for it, out the side and over the edge. Trailers in the north corner will try to crawl across the trough toward the south, striving for the light. Spend a few moments now and then to train them over their intended edge. It is always thriving plants that consent to spill abundantly over the side of their containers—so keep them thriving.

Crossover ground covers

A second category of droolers are the miniature ground covers that have run out of real estate. *Artemisia caucasica* is a soft, silver, velvet carpet that will hit the edge of the trough and continue over. *Veronica rupestris* and *V. repens* 'Sunshine' will, too. The close mat of *Globularia repens* will take time to get to the edge, but then continues downward, although this will take more than one season.

Lithodora diffusa is an enchantress, luring you in with the true blue of the best gentians. Once she claims you, there is no listening to the voice of reason that says how finicky and exacting she is. No matter what heroics you are driven to with lithodora, she only seems to become smaller and weaker after a few seasons. Some years the cascade goes on blooming forever, and all seems right with the world. But sooner than later, you will have to replace her. *Lithodora oleifolia* is a less intense blue, the flowers paler. They emerge pink and age to blue in the manner of mertensias. The habit is tufted, a hummock instead of a mat; the undersides of the leaves are silky and silver. This one does not have the magnetic pull of her sister, but she is a touch more reliable and less the drama queen.

Thymes are classic spilling out of a container, sometimes reaching the ground below, and have been known to root down there, too, and begin to make a patch. All very picturesque. Be cautious, though: thymes are thugs in a trough. Remember that the plant you see above the ground is only half the story. The root space they take up is the other half.

Lithodora oleifolia.

Crossover cushions

These never waterfall with abandon over the side. Conjure up an image of an old-fashioned shaving cup filled with shaving cream. The shaving cream sort of billows up and foams over the edge. That's exactly what certain cushion plants will do, but they can take more than a season to get there. The three microphloxes—*Phlox subulata* 'Betty', 'Herbert', and 'Sileniflora'—will do this. Given a couple years, asperulas (with their soft, tubular flowers) and *Androsace* 'Millstream' will perform the shaving cup trick, too.

SUCCULENTS

Cactus

Though it often surprises people, there are many cold-hardy cactus species. Two genera small enough to dwell in troughs are *Echinocereus* and *Coryphantha*. There are lots of named forms. *Echinocereus reichenbachii* is only a few inches high with an eventual two-inch diameter, flowering in a purple-pink. Although I am dedicated to promoting the use of botanical Latin, once in a while I find a soft spot in my heart for a common name, and that of E. *reichenbachii*—lace hedgehog cactus—is one of those. Another in the same genus is E. *triglochidiatus*, densely spiny and bearing large red flowers. Then there is E. *triglochidiatus* var. *inermis*. A mouthful to be sure, but the variety name tells us that it is unarmed or without spines. Cactus lovers pay lots of attention to the spines on their plants; the color can be dramatic, the patterns intricate. Then what, exactly, does a spineless cactus have to offer? Well, it will not stab you. And it is just plain cute. *Coryphantha vivipara* (sometimes found in the genus *Escobaria*) is another pink one. Its attractive spines are in a star-shaped array. *Coryphantha sulcata* offers golden spines and bronzy yellow blooms. Its blossoms are showstoppers.

Keep in mind that as they mature, many dwarf cactus species can form interesting "waistlines" around the column. Some species form pups, not always at the base, but sometimes higher up, in the form of "arms."

Assigning a zone to cacti is tough because they are xeric. Cold is not the only issue; winter wet also comes into play. Many are listed as being hardy to zone 4 and 5 in some sources, but from experience I know they are hardy to at least zone 6. Some described above are commonly called ball cactus, eventually forming clusters.

I like cactus grown by themselves in a trough, or mixed with other succulents. They seem to look at home. It is also easier to meet their needs by keeping things simple. Place troughs with these prickly inhabitants where they will suffer less weed incursion, away from weed-infested verges. This is experience talking: weeding a cactus trough is less than fun, and I have yet to find gloves that protect you from all spines.

Coryphantha sulcata.

Delosperma 'Alan's Apricot'.

Delospermas

The always-lengthening list of ice plants in the trade seems to include a hot new one or new series every year. They come in a rainbow of colors, the flat, iridescent daisies plentiful and long blooming. Some are more cold hardy than others, some more tolerant of moisture. Ice plant flowers close up when the sun is not shining, so design accordingly. *Delosperma alpina* is a rare little jewel, with small white flowers spangling a mat of foliage so dark an oxblood-red as to appear black. It will occasionally go summer dormant. *Delosperma congestum* and its cultivars 'Gold Nugget' and 'White Nugget' are hardy and reliable. *Delosperma nubigenum* has been around for a long while and is cold hardy, draping extensively over the side of a trough after a season or two. *Delosperma ashtonii* 'Blut' is sturdy enough for green roofs. It is a good grower, with bright purple blooms.

Jovibarbas

Jovibarbas are the forgotten succulent, sometimes lumped into that catchall, hens and chicks. Easygoing *Jovibarba hirta* varieties are known as rollers because that is what they do. Babies form on top of mature clusters of rosettes and, at the barest touch (I suspect the patter of rain can release them), they detach and roll off to root wherever conditions are amenable.

A *Jovibarba heuffellii* cultivar with lime-green leaves, paired with coryphantha and chunks of tufa.

When we turn to *Jovibarba heuffelii* plants, affectionately known as the huffies, we have entered glamorous territory. Which is why it is bewildering to me that they are so little known. I would love these for one reason alone: their colors become *more* vibrant as summer wears on. Think about that for a minute. How often have you acquired succulents in general and sempervivums in particular, only to have them go all greeny-bronzy on you by August, if not sooner? Adding huffies to your succulent planting will spice it up. To tempt the aficionado there is *J. heuffelii* 'Sunny Side Up', gold to green at the base with vermillion tips blushing more intensely as the season proceeds. 'Apache' is chocolate-cherry color, 'Zorongo' an earthy Indian red. Many cultivars display distinct, cream-colored pencil lines circumscribing the edge of each leaf, an enchanting feature. 'Gold Bug' and 'Orange Tip' are self-explanatory.

A *Jovibarba heuffelii* selection with red tips, next to *Orostachys iwarenge* in center.

Orostachys

These are sometimes included under hen and chicks, too. Best known is the opaque gray to putty-colored one often called dunce cap. It arrives under two names: *Orostachys iwarenge* and *O. furusei*. The gray mixes wonderfully with other tones. Remove pups and stick them to root around the mother plant if you are intent on keeping a colony going. If all rosettes flower, you will lose the whole plant.

The color of *Orostachys malacophylla* is like that of a Granny Smith apple. It has waxy rosettes that are winter dormant. *Orostachys spinosa* and *O. minuta* have spines at the leaf tips. These plants are very slow to increase and if gastropods get at them, a cluster can be destroyed in one night.

Also under the umbrella of hens and chicks are species of *Rosularia*. Most are small to medium sized, with great texture. Some names to look for are *R. chrysantha*, *R. platyphylla*, and the stunning *R. rosulata* and *R. serpentinica*.

Sedums

Sedum hispanicum var. *minus* has fine texture that looks attractive near larger succulents. It will spill over the edge and in intense sun, will turn up the charm with a gray that is kissed with blue, lavender, or pink. The colors are nuanced. *Sedum album* 'Coral Carpet' has tiny leaves like jelly beans that turn cranberry color in the winter.

Rosularia rosulata.

It is easy to fall for the several forms of *S. spathulifolium*: 'Cape Blanco' is so silver as to appear bright white, 'Harvest Moon' is a similar coloration, and 'Carnea' is a stunning fleshy pink with overtones of purple in more sun. I find these hard to keep because of winter wetness, but also hard to resist. They are very brittle and break easily. A favorite is *Sedum* 'Borchii Sport'. Another jelly bean type, this one will form crests. The stems thicken and widen, and the leaves cluster into a cockscomb that will cascade—a lot of dazzle for a little supporting player. *Sedum dasyphyllum* 'Minor', gray green and soft looking, is sturdier than its sibling *S. dasyphyllum* 'Major', which seems to have meltdown troubles during humid summers. When thriving, though, it will draw all eyes; its cushion of fatter leaves approaches a turquoise blue.

Sempervivums

These are the most well-known hens and chicks. Blooms tend to disappoint, forming big, juicy columns with starry little flowers that always result in the death of the rosette producing them. *Sempervivum arachnoideum* flowers are a little prettier than most, bearing pink to salmon-colored blooms. The gardener has to learn to manage the blossoms on succulents like these, lest they bloom out and the plant falls apart. Cutting off the flowering stem will not stop the loss of the rosette. Try to acquire ones that bloom sparingly, and do not overfertilize. Once the plant has flowered, twist the column off the plant and use baby pups to fill in any space, if needed.

Sempervivums with *Sedum* 'Borchii Sport'.

Sempervivums can be found as straight species such as *S. tectorum*, which is also the progenitor of many cultivated varieties, as are *S. calcareum* and *S. ciliosum*. However, it is the rich array of stunning named cultivars that bewitches the collector and the casual gardener every time. It seems foolish to even try to assemble a short list. It would be like picking out a flavor of ice cream for someone at the counter of a shop with one of those long, enticing menus. You really should just go to the counter and decide for yourself.

THE SHADE TROUGH

The shade trough is an entirely different creature than one designed for sun. The plant vocabulary for shade is much, much shorter. The plants are not even alpines: since there is no timber above timberline, there is no appreciable cover. Shade plants that are in scale with the small landscape offer a few options. But a deep shade situation might not be the best place to plan a trough garden. Make peace with the idea that a trough for shade will never have the same look as one for sun. Since the shade plants will usually have a leafier look, and generally be taller eventually, I suggest

Mixed sempervivum bowl with *Antennaria* 'Nyewoods'.

staging it a little differently, too. Take a tip from the Zen beauty of the moss garden, allow for some open space mulched with quiet gravel. Select plants for leaf interest, fall in love with the stones you use to bring architecture to the plant-up. Design for dramatic impact—not always easy, as many shade subjects are more bashful.

Shrubs for shade

Although boxwoods do well in sun, I turn to *Buxus microphylla* 'Kingsville', the smallest boxwood, more often for a shade trough, maybe because it is unexpected. A shiny, tiny-leaved, evergreen, woody cushion, it is also immanently shearable, allowing the gardener to carve out a shape or reduce its size. It will be many years before 'Kingsville' will need reduction, though, if ever.

Depending on your climate, *Chamaecyparis* species, especially those cultivars with golden or white-tipped foliage, often prefer less sun. Many "golds" are slow growing and take on charming chartreuse tones in shade.

Cryptomeria japonica 'Twinkle Toes', though it labors under a silly name, is pretty, with new growth that is a soft gold against the dark green of the previous year's foliage. The foliage is incredibly dense and the growth habit adorably irregular: chubby, but with peaks and valleys. The sunnier side of the plant gets a heavier dusting of variegation, looking like golden snow. Since it will scorch in too much sun, best to give it open shade or only a bit of morning sun.

Picea is another genus for very light shade. Stick to the smallest, listed as "dwarf," or even better, "miniature."

Tsuga is a classic genus for shade. Some forms are tiny and mounded, others upright. There is the weeping *Tsuga canadensis* 'Cole's Prostrate' and the beautiful *Tsuga diversifolia* 'Loowit'. Both have lovely bright green spring growth; the latter has a layered look.

Other shade plants

Acorus gramineus 'Minimus Aureus' is the tiniest sweet flag, at three inches high. It bleaches in too much sun and likes a bit of moisture. The deeper the shade, the more chartreuse it will be. Near stones it forms a bright spot, a golden fringe that shines across the garden.

Alchemilla alpina and *A. faroensis* are the smallest lady's mantles. Leafy fans are deeply cut, with silver backs and edges. Bloom is barely an event, consisting of tiny greenish yellow flowers in sprays. A great supporting player.

Asplenium trichomanes is a nice foliage specimen for even deep shade. Also known as maidenhair spleenwort, it is delicate looking but pretty tough once established.

The *Astilbe* Cobblewood Series is a terrific breakthrough for trough gardeners. When in flower, plants are about five inches, their crinkly basal foliage is much shorter. 'Fireworks' is first to bloom: a deep, bright pink exploding in typical astilbe flowerheads. 'Cotton Candy' is next, exactly the color of the sugary treat at the county fair and just as fluffy. 'Shooting Stars' is white and latest to bloom.

Heuchera pulchella, and *H. rubescens*, at around two inches leaf height, are trough worthy. Both have pale pink flowers and a handsome base of rounded leaves. *Heuchera abramsii* is a bit smaller with darker blooms.

Hosta venusta, the classic miniature, has heart-shaped green leaves topped in summer by light purple flowers. Count on this choice to be a good clumper. Two beautiful variegated hostas are *H.* 'Cameo', and the much-beloved *H.* 'Pandora's Box'.

Venerable old *Buxus microphylla* 'Kingsville' in company with *Rhododendron* 'Wren' (yellow flowers), *Acorus gramineus* 'Minimus Aureus' between the rocks, *Lewisia longipetala* 'Little Mango' (orange flowers), and *Lindernia grandiflora* in front. Both troughs contain *Hosta* 'Pandora's Box'; the small trough has a miniature tsuga.

Two *Astilbe* Cobblewood Series 'Fireworks' specimens. *Chamaecyparis* 'Golden Fern' is the anchor plant to the left.

Lysimachia japonica var. *minutissima*

Green and either cream or white leaves add drama. The oddly named *H.* 'Giantland Sunny Mouse Ears' is a winner if you want solid gold; it also has an iridescent quality. Maxing out at three inches tall, it can spread to ten inches. This cultivar harkens from the 'Mouse Ears' line of pygmy hostas, and like them, it has solid substance and a classy poise in the way each leaf is held. If you are a fan of mini hostas, the entire 'Mouse ears' pedigree will provide many great choices.

Lysimachia japonica var. *minutissima* is reliable as a very flat, green ground cover with tiny yellow stars sprayed over the carpet in late spring. But I suggest this plant with two warnings. It not only can but most likely will be invasive, not just in your trough, but anywhere in your garden it pleases. I had it leap to the other side of the house. The only situation I can think of that would cause this is the use of leaf blowers in the fall dispersing the seed. It is in the rock garden now, entrenched. But it is pretty, and very useful for shade. The other possible deal-breaker is that it greens up very late in the spring, so late that you will be convinced you lost it. Until it comes bounding back, in more places than you thought possible.

Ophiopogon japonicus 'Pygmaeus' is a three-inch-tall mondo grass with deep green blades. The surprise comes when you see the berries: they are blue. Not any old gardener's "almost" or "bluish grayish green." They are deep and bright and exactly the color of blue M&M's.

Viola pedata, a North American native also known as the bird's foot violet.

Ramonda is a queenly genus for the partial shade trough. There are three species: *R. myconi*, *R. nathaliae*, and *R. serbica*; the first is the most available. They like being planted vertically or in some sort of crevice and resent too much winter wetness. It is nothing short of astonishing to watch leaves of these plants reawaken at the onset of spring. The winter-browned and somewhat crispy leaves undergo a greening transformation. The brittle leafage returns to quilted emerald vitality. Blooms of ramondas remind one of African violets. The two are in fact related; both are members of the family Gesneriaceae. Flowers range from white to pink to lilac, the latter being the most common. The related genus *Haberlea* is another to seek out, though it is a little harder to find.

Thalictrum kiusianum, despite its airy look, is a workhorse in a shade trough. Four-inch stems emerge above lacy leaves. Its blossoms are recognizably those of a meadow rue, forming lavender clouds of fringy flowers. This long-blooming favorite will form a colony in time.

Violets are another group to plumb for shade candidates. If you are drawn to *Viola pedata*, known as the bird's foot violet, it must have dryish conditions and more sunlight than most other violets—not a good choice for heavy shade. It is a lovely North American native with deeply dissected foliage.

Viola koreana.

Violets seem to have two speeds: drop dead or unstoppable. In other words, there are a lot of violets that just aren't hardy. And there are a bunch that are pretty hellishly invasive. I succumbed to a sweet one called 'Freckles', whose pale blue flower petals are heavily speckled and spotted in deep china-blue. Be forewarned—it seeds everywhere. And by everywhere, I mean in the center of a hosta, on top of iris rhizomes, and in the lawn.

I have a soft spot for *Viola koreana*. It can be found under several names, including *V. coreana* and *V. gyprocerus*, and may be garnished with variety or cultivar names such as *exilis* and 'Sylettas'. This is an Asian species also known as the cyclamen-leafed violet. Its silver leaf variegation is intricate and similar in shape and size to cyclamen leaves. Now, to its proclivities. It will self-sow but is not permanent, and moves about in its own inscrutable way, daring you to keep it in place anywhere. There used to be a big, healthy colony of this plant in one quadrant of a large trough that had persisted for many years. I got the itch to propagate it, which can be done by seed quite easily, but I had neglected to collect any. So, trowel in hand, I went and lifted a little patch out of what was dozens if not hundreds of violets of many ages and stages. I disturbed things as little as possible. By the next spring, all trace of *V. koreana* had vanished from that trough. It was as though I had dequeened the hive, and the workers had swarmed off.

Aquilegia scopulorum.

CORRALLING THE REST

There are always plants that resist being categorized, which just makes our gardening life more interesting. Here are some genera a trough gardener would not want to live without, and within that, a species or two worth noting.

Aquilegias that are small and choice deserve a place in our troughs. *Aquilegia jonesii* is a stunner, but never seems to flower well in captivity. If you see this in the mountains, you will not believe the flower color, a deep icy blue. Its lacy, turquoise to silver huddle of foliage makes it ultimately worth growing without any flowers at all. Finding plants can be a challenge, tracking down seed is a little easier. *Aquilegia scopulorum* is worth growing, too. It is a little bigger and is distinguished by the incredibly long, beautiful spurs on its flowers. The plant can vary in size and color; most are some variation of blue and white. Both these species are natives of the American West.

Xanthisma coloradoensis used to be found in the genus *Aster* but is now assigned to *Xanthisma*. I don't know if I will ever make peace with the reasons botanists change names like this. Taxonomy has been undergoing a gigantic upheaval of late, which we can blame on the use of DNA to reclassify the system. A few years ago, I attended a lecture by a scientist who waxed euphoric on the blessing of DNA testing to reassign plants, as the audience generally grew more wary and sober. Especially those of us who work in this industry. At one point, a very knowledgeable listener had a question. "Once you've got everything tested and reassigned, will that finally be the end of it?" (The audience grumbled its assent.) "Well," said the speaker after a pause, "You must understand, it is not that simple." What we as an audience understood was simple enough: that a bunch of scientists seem unwilling to quit worrying at all the names we have come to depend on, and find another so-called problem to solve. When I started learning botanical Latin twenty-three years ago, I found it exciting. Learning yet another new name assigned to a plant I know and love for the third or fourth time is just disheartening. And having species kicked out of their families is even worse!

Anyway, back to *Xanthisma coloradoensis*. It has lovely mid-pink daisies, as any self-respecting aster should, and grayish green tuffets of leaves. After a first flush of bloom, if deadheaded, it will, on its own quirky timetable, toss out flowers again now and then.

Astragalus and *Oxytropis*—ah, the locoweeds! I will treat these genera together as they have similar attributes and foibles. Some are too large for trough culture. They are westerners for the most part and have long roots that want to go deep. *Astragalus utahensis* is bright silver with rose-colored pea flowers. *Astragalus barrii* is another charmer of a perfect size. Of the many *Oxytopis* choices, I would select *O. multiceps*. It is choice and small, with bewitching silky silver leaves and pink blooms.

These two genera have some of the most ravishing silver foliage you could ever want in an alpine, worth growing for that feature alone. The blossoms are often quite large for the size of the plant and come in colors from white to pink, purple, red purple, and bi-tones. The foibles start with cultivation. These plants need tons of sun and limited moisture, including low humidity. They are also the absolute first choice of gastropods everywhere. Every slug and snail within a quarter mile will gallop (well, they would if they had feet) to reach these delectable plants. I have never understood why the toxins in locoweeds do not seem to affect their attackers. Maybe I just don't have the sensitivity necessary to recognize when a slug has gone loco. Cattle

Astragalus barrii.

Campanula chamissonis.

famously die from these plants, and apparently display crazy behavior beforehand. I have never seen a slug or snail fall victim to the same fate. They don't just sample the leaves, either, they eat them right down to the ground. All that remains will be the sticky silver trails of the enemy, slinking off somewhere to smugly digest his lunch.

Campanulas are neither cushion, cascader, nor ground cover in many cases, though they can display traits of all three. Like cushions, some will mound up in the spring before flowering. Many also increase vegetatively underground as ground covers do. The problem with campanulas in troughs is that most of the growable ones are too vigorous; the ones that will stay in scale are hard to find, hard to grow, and hard to keep. This is another race that must be protected from slugs and snails. They will even cross a piece of copper tape and make their slimy way over gravel to get to a choice campanula. *Campanula chamissonis* is a winner and amenable to cultivation. Its deciduous, glossy foliage produces tubby bells on short stems. The blossoms usually have a white center.

Collomia debilis is a beautiful plant that is rare in the trade. The leaves, tufted and sticky, form a mound or mat. The flowers are upward-facing cups and are variable, ranging from pale to strong pinks and lilacs. It is easy to grow from seed if you can find it.

Erigeron aureus 'Canary Bird' is a choice little fleabane, with soft yellow daisies over dark green tufts of leaves. Descriptions don't do it justice; even those who will not let a yellow bloom inside their gate always soften on this one. *Erigeron* 'Goat

Erigeron 'Canary Bird'.

Rocks' is another fine yellow-flowered specimen. *Erigeron leiomerus* has buds that emerge on crooked stems that look like tiny swan necks. They eventually open facing upward, a strong medium lavender color. So many alpine daisies end up looking washed out. These three have outstanding color.

Certain gentians offer us blooms of such a saturated azure that they have become the color against which all other blues are judged. It can be heart stopping. There are very few naturally occurring true blues in nature. Most so-called blue flowers—think bellflowers, balloon flowers, catnip, sage, even clematis—are some variation of mauve, lavender, or violet; beautiful colors in their own right, but not really blue. The bloom of *Gentiana acaulis* is genuinely cobalt. It is the color of the best grade of lapis ever found. For me, this plant is happier in a trough than in the ground, with a couple of provisos. Gentians are heavy feeders. They seem to like disturbed soil. What this adds up to is a gorgeous plant that does best when it is up- or repotted at least every other year. When it begins to produce only small leaves it will cease to

Gentiana acaulis.

Gentiana verna.

flower, a telltale sign that action is required. This makes it hard to design with it in a trough. My solution has been to grow it alone in a monoculture planting. Failing that, try to keep the roommates few and simple, so resetting and refreshing the soil of the gentian is still possible.

Gentiana boissieri is a bit smaller than the above, and well behaved. The blue is more purple; it can be hard to find a source. Seed is the best option. *Gentiana verna* is the other gentian everybody wants. A spectacular alpine, never really a permanent feature in any planting, it seems to have a life span of a few years. Year one or two may have you crowing that you've cracked the *G. verna* code. Take a picture. Take many. Come talk to me a couple years later. But it is still worth planting, worth replacing, worth, at the very least, the photos and the bragging rights. There are many other gentians to explore, including some from the Himalaya that are not easy to acquire and even harder to grow and keep.

Named after Lewis of Lewis and Clark fame, *Lewisia* plants are an odd tribe to categorize. The leaves of lewisias are indeed succulent, but they can't be shoved into the hurly burly of a typical succulent planting. Their needs are more exacting, not to mention the fleshy taproot that needs deep soil. These plants are sometimes placed in lists for shade. Although it is true they do not want to live on a sunny sand dune, too much shade can contribute to their decline. Once root rot sets in, there is little to be done. They do not like excessive water, especially at the crown. Some species within the genus seem more prone to this, I would single out *L. cotyledon* as the most vulnerable of the bunch. While it is a beauty queen to be sure, I would nonetheless steer clear of *Lewisia cotyledon*, as it has the worst record for longevity.

I would also caution those new to lewisias to approach the desirable *Lewisia tweedyi* and *Lewisia rediviva* with a lot of respect and lowered expectations. Both bear superb flowers, but can be difficult and cranky about too much humidity, moisture, heat, and winter wetness.

Any *Lewisia* species will need at least eight inches of depth, with no real room for negotiating. A favorite is *Lewisia columbiana* and its varieties. It is a solidly perennial evergreen, with a rosette that will slowly accrue more rosettes, until you have a handsome cluster. Its flowers have a baby's breath effect, delicate and dancing above basal leaves on thin, many-branched stems. Blooms range from white to pink to cerise; they are small, do not expect the huge flowers found in other members of the clan. *L. columbiana* is a survivor and a performer, and it packs a lot of charm.

The other group to consider is the one made up of hybrid crosses between *Lewisia cotyledon* and *L. longipetala*. Neither species is that easy to grow, but with bloodlines intermingled, the resultant plants display that cliché known as "hybrid vigor." *Lewisia longipetala* × *cotyledon* 'Little Plum' started the whole thing. Smaller than *L. cotyledon* but as evergreen as its parent, it bears large pink to purple flowers and is amenable to trough cultivation. *Lewisia longipetala* 'Little Peach' came next. Similar in size and shape, it has a great record of returning after winter. Its flowers look like smaller blooms of *Lewisia tweedyi*. That alone is recommendation aplenty to seek it out. Then along came 'Little Mango' with, well, mango-colored flowers. Newest to arrive is 'Little Raspberry'. And at least so far, that completes the trough-friendly fruit salad.

Penstemon is an extraordinary race of ornamental plants, a North American genus that runs the gamut from tiny to immense, both in plant stature and flower size. Rock and trough gardeners have a lot of material to wade through. It would be easy to simply focus on the smallest ones and call our homework done. But these plants need to be rated on garden-worthy performance for those of us who do not live in the native haunts of penstemons. Different nativity means different growing requirements. The tiny western treasures such as *P. acaulis* and *P. yampaensis* (to bracket the alphabet) are stunning. They will capture your heart irretrievably and bring on a covetous attack in the most mild-mannered rock gardener. All I can say is, trying to find them is difficult in and of itself; keeping them for even part of one season is an accomplishment. If you live in Colorado or Utah, there may be more hope.

Penstemon davidsonii.

Polygala chamaebuxus 'Rhodoptera'.

Shaking off the impossible dream, let's evaluate a few penstemons that may actually live for more than seventeen minutes. Of the shrubby pents, *Penstemon rupicola* will have the effect of a small shrub in a trough. *Penstemon cardwellii* is a similar species to seek out; there is a lovely white form one sees from time to time. At around ten inches in height, it may need a bigger trough. *Penstemon davidsonii* is a great low-growing choice.

In the realm of non-shrubby pents, I will plug *Penstemon hirsutus* var. *pygmaeus*. With tufted leaves that are deep purple in cold weather, it bursts into a fluffy wedding cake of lilac and white flowers later in spring. A permanent and easygoing plant. Not tiny, and yes, it will probably self-sow. But you may also get a gift of some pretty variations; a good rose-pink and whites are not unknown. The other not-tiny pent I urge you to try is *Penstemon hallii*. From strappy basal leaves, flower stalks rise six or so inches with gorgeous blooms of violet blue. With age, the base can become woody. *Penstemon procerus* var. *formosus* has thick leaves clustering into patches. It blooms on three-inch stems in deep blue violet. These are just a few of the choices. There is a whole society devoted to penstemons for good reason.

*Potentilla
porphyrantha.*

Polygala chamaebuxus 'Rhodoptera' is a little evergreen shrublet, six inches high with waxy oval leaves. There are a few other species, but to my eye this is the one to get. It behaves perennially. Flowers are a striking bi-tone of rose purple and yellow. Polygalas are known for suckering, forming a colony eventually. Time is the key—and patience. By patience, I mean that I urge you to not attempt to divide or take cuttings of this plant too soon; let your patch become well established first.

Potentilla hyparctica 'Nana' is a classic silver-leaved cinquefoil bearing yellow flowers. It sometimes seeds around gently, which is welcome, as the plants are not particularly long lived. *Potentilla verna* 'Orange Flame' is reliably perennial with lush emerald foliage and typical bright yellow blooms. The queen of the tribe (also the most miffy) is *Potentilla nitida*, and it can usually be had only by sowing seed. The photos of silvery mats crowned by large glowing pink blossoms will steal your heart. It is quite possible to germinate it, and even to grow it on for a few seasons, but it simply doesn't seem to flower well under the ministrations of humans. Lucky for trough gardeners, though, and relatively new on the scene, we have *Potentilla porphyrantha*. It provides a silver mat and a peach-pink batch of blooms on branching stems that actually continue for a while, cool weather permitting. It also sets seed well in captivity and seems to have staying power, along with all that charm.

Scabiosa japonica var. *alpina* 'Ritz Blue' with *Lewisia longipetala* 'Little Tutti Frutti', *Lindernia grandiflora*, and *Sempervivum* Chick Charms 'Gold Nugget'.

I confess to growing *Scabiosa japonica* var. *alpina* 'Ritz Blue' lean. It has come back reliably for three years, so far. The best features are little pincushion blooms throughout the season. It may take a break during the really hot span in summer, but if deadheaded now and then, it will rebloom again. The leaves are dark green tufts, the blossoms are dark lavender.

I have a soft spot for a few *Teucrium* species that I cannot justify. They live a few years at best, and are not exactly splashy. Nonetheless, there is just something appealing about them. I used to be able to find one under the name *T. ackermannii*, now sometimes listed as a form of *T. polium*, a decumbent subshrub with narrow velvety leaves and red purple flower heads; *T. aroanium* is another semi-woody mat former. This one has white felting on the stems and undersides of the leaves, along with soft purple blooms.

PLANTING STYLES

B EYOND THE WELL-LOVED MINIATURE landscape style covered in the planting chapter, here are a few other interesting design ideas.

THE SUCCULENT BOWL

A trug-shaped trough planted as a landscape. Clockwise from upper left: mugo pine seedling with thyme beneath, *Lonicera crassifolia* in golden flower, *Orostachys spinosa*, *Echinocereus reichenbachii* subsp. *perbellus* 'Red Top Ranch', *Coryphantha vivipara*, a patch of silver *Raoulia australis*, and a very young *Salvia daghestanica*. *Sedum grisebachii* fills the gorge inside the tufa canyon.

Hardy succulents are riding a popular wave these days, and succulents planted in a big wide bowl seem to strike a chord. You don't need to stick with the bowl shape, either, though it is classic. It is especially interesting to use a shallow trough in an unexpected free-form shape with succulents. Generally, this type of design does not include rocks, nor does it depend on an upright anchor plant. It is simply a mosaic of texture, shape, and color. This is one time when it's fine to leave very little gravel showing and to carpet the space with plants. After years of doing succulent plant-ups, I have a few guidelines:

CONTRAST THE SIZE OF THE ROSETTES. It is almost always more balanced to have a few giant artichokes (or even medium ones) and a greater number of small ones.

DON'T PLACE YOUR FEATURED, OR LARGEST, SUCCULENT DEAD CENTER. The design will feel static.

WORK ON MIXING UP THE TEXTURES. Blend fine with plump and waxy or satiny with felted or cobwebbed.

HAVE A SMALL-LEAVED SEDUM SOFTENING THE EDGE, SPILLING OVER.

Succulents in various shapes.

This is (or should be) pure play. Nothing is at stake here except maybe your afternoon, so have some fun. Try clashing colors—or marry them. For contrast, try gold or silver with burgundy. To blend the colors, do a subtle monochromatic mix with tones of gray shading to lilac, blue, and rose; make some flat and opaque, some reflective or opalescent. This palette can be as rich and rewarding as the contrasted colors.

Newbies often hesitantly ask if can they have flowers in their succulent trough. The answer is, of course—they are just not usually featured players. One advantage of succulents is that unlike flowering plants, these slow growers kind of stay the same all season. There will be growth, there will be a few blooms, but generally they will look good all the time.

Three baguettes
displaying different
color themes.

An arrangement of cuttings

This is a variation on the succulent trough in that it uses mostly succulents, but depends upon small cuttings for a large portion of its design. It's not meant to last forever because those same cuttings may outgrow their space and thus their usefulness in a year or so. But it is also easily refurbished as the mood strikes. A cuttings trough is meant to grace an outdoor table or counter, or perhaps the top of a wall, almost like a floral arrangement that lasts all season or longer. Cuttings can be assembled in any trough shape, but a winning form is what I call the baguette, because it's longer than it is wide and is rounded at the ends. It can be narrow and slender, impressively large, or anything in between. Many hardy succulents root easily; a new plant can be made from just a small sprig from the mother plant. This, by the way, is a great reason to have succulents planted in various parts of the garden—they become a source of cutting material when the irrepressible urge to create hits you.

Choose some feature succulents for their foliage color and texture. A favorite combination of mine is gold and silver. Once combined, these tones sing. I believe it is because within the gold and silver in plant leaves are the ghosts of two other colors that famously harmonize: yellow and blue. Gardener's gold often leans pleasantly

Aside from the cacti, these two arrangements are filled with cuttings.

into chartreuse and there is blue seeping through many silver plants leaves. So be fearless with your foliage colors. By the way, flowers can spoil the profile of this trough design, I have been known to cut off the stems as soon as they emerge, well ahead of flowering.

Symmetry actually works rather well in this style. Usually I select a cluster of large rosettes for the centerpiece. *Sempervivum* 'Royanum' and *S. calcareum* 'Sir William Lawrence' are both bold and big, green based with beautiful tip markings. For a muted palette, consider the lovely gray-silver-rose-lavender of *S.* 'Lilac Time'. The dark grape-colored heart of *S. tectorum* 'Atroviolaceum' is another strong option. There are many others, including the fabulous *Jovibarba heuffelii* cultivars. For fine-textured leaves, consider the same choices as for the succulent bowl: tiny sedums, perhaps a thyme, a tight dianthus, or an antennaria to break things up. Usually I choose a secondary rosette player in a smaller size. The selections of *S. arachnoideum* are particularly nice as an addition when there is a satiny or watermarked central semp. *Sempervivum arachnoideum* 'Cobweb Joy' is nice and tight and webby, for example.

Once the main players are in place, it is time to free the florist in you. First, grit the trough, taking care to mulch around the crowns plus any blank areas. Get out a pencil or a chopstick and a pair of scissors. Then just have fun—take cuttings of any succulents that please you and will root (the one exception being any, like the huffies—*Jovibarba heuffelii*—that need to be sliced and calloused before they will root). If you want longevity from this trough, then select only the smaller, slower-growing options. But don't be afraid to step out of that box. There is an exciting new range of sedums with leaves in rosy wine tones. They should be fair game, even if they may outgrow their place. You can always redo their spot next year! And don't neglect older beauties. I am still an avid fan of *Sedum cauticola* and its varieties. Pilfer a few stems of the exotic *Sedum sieboldii* 'Mediovariegatum'. This compelling creature has deep cream leaves edged in a gray that is slamming hard into turquoise. That in turn is edged in brick red. This plant can fight aesthetically with others, but when a combination works it is triumphant. Play to its cream and blue-greens and you will hit a home run.

Taking cuttings

When you take a cutting, remove a leaf or two or three from the bottom of the stem, poke a hole in the grit where you want it to grow, insert the cutting, and gently firm it in with a couple of fingers of both hands. That's all there is to it. It usually works best visually to cluster a number of cuttings of the same species together in a spot. This gives the pattern an abundant look. Use contrast to the hilt here. If your central rosettes are purple, tuck gold cuttings near them. If you have gone maverick and decided that *Ophiopogon planiscapus* 'Nigrescens' (black mondo grass) shall be your centerpiece, then clash it well with something bold.

The last sprigs I add make me feel like a chef garnishing a platter. This is the moment I turn to *Sedum* 'Borchii Sport'. It is another small jelly bean–like sedum that becomes crested at maturity, and even cascades over the side. Add a few more of these adornments than you think necessary, as a couple of rootings may fail. Since you are working with cuttings, there is an optimum time frame for doing this. Early to midspring will give you the highest success rate for rooting; toward the end of August is the latest you should attempt it. Be mindful of watering the first few weeks. Also consider placing the trough in a protected, slightly less sunny spot until your cuttings strike and grow away before placing it in its permanent home.

A mirror-image plant-up featuring repetition of *Dianthus freynii*, rooted cuttings of *Thuja* 'Rheingold', *Sempervivum* 'Royanum', and *Cotula* 'Platt's Black'.

THE JEKYLL BORDER TROUGH

This reference to Gertrude Jekyll's hallmark flower borders is probably too grand for a trough planting design, but it makes a point. Not a landscape or a mosaic, this method is unique in the way it is built of repeating textures, colors, and shapes. The best herbaceous borders are often ones that rhythmically repeat a few elements down the length of the bed. Repetition depends on the linear area you have to work with. To accomplish this result in a trough requires using a long container, at least twice as long as it is wide. Longer is even better, more of the window box shape. The repetition can come from using the same plant a number of times or, as an interesting alternative, simply repeating the same color of foliage. Repetition can even work when using a muted monochromatic color scheme, as long as you vary and repeat several distinct shapes and textures. Think of velvety, smooth, and spiky, just for starters.

Before getting underway, decide where this piece will live. Location will determine if it will be viewed largely from one side, from both, or even, if on a table,

Affectionately known as "the olive dish," this trough features a repeated plant and rock pattern.

Silver, gold, and green textures in a striated canyon trough. *Sedum sieboldii* 'Mediovariegatum' is on the left.

in the round. If only one side will be seen, then lavish your artistry there; if both sides will be visible, you may want to repeat elements on both sides if the trough is wide enough to do so. It is nice to be able to use a plant three times, especially if it's a major element.

Repeating a series of beautiful rocks, all of the same type, is unexpected and visually captivating. Use chunks of rock that are bigger and taller than you imagine will work. This trough evolves over the season by burgeoning. Make sure the rocks will show even then. Genuine tufa rock is gorgeous used this way.

In my own window box troughs, I generally insist on a few cascaders repeated down the length. This adds movement and another dimension to the entire piece. If the trough is meant to be viewed from all sides and you add droolers only to one side, it will feel lopsided, so add one to each side for symmetry, or plant the two sides as

A meatball trough filled with beach stones and planted asymmetrically with *Santolina chamaecyparissus* 'Small Ness', *Echinocereus reichenbachii* subsp. *perbellus* 'Red Top Ranch', *Coryphantha sulcata*, and *Orostachys iwarenge* tucked among the stones.

mirror images. Simply start in the middle and work outward both ways, alternating sides. For example, cascaders can spill down the right and left sides, but they don't need to be exactly lined up to a center axis. In the case of mirror image planting, it helps to place your pots of plants before beginning to install them. There is no rule that says that you must repeat slavishly. Choose plants that rhyme with each other by color, shape, or texture, and the planting will be cohesive. There is also no rule that says you cannot be asymmetrical, or that you cannot graduate colors of foliage in some way—starting dark, for instance, and ending pale, or starting large and sizing down to small.

Mini urns at the base of a planter, with metal and sandstone spheres.

MONOCULTURE

A ridiculously easy style of planting troughs is monoculture. You select a trough of appropriate size for a single plant. There are a couple of reasons to do this. One big one is to care for and protect a rare alpine. Monoculture means a smaller trough, which usually means a portable situation—so you can shift the plant to more sun or less depending on time of year. You can also place it near your door where it is in sight, so tending is automatic. If this is a gentian or a lewisia, for instance, it will

A collection of miniature hostas.

Triple triangles—with *Sedum nevii*, garnished with *Sempervivum tectorum* 'Atroviolaceum' (left), and *Antennaria dioica* 'Nyewoods Variety' garnished with *Sempervivum* 'Lilac Time'. In front, a mussel shell trough with *Dianthus squarrosus*.

Not monoculture, but an ingenious statement on trough planting style. Meet Brigitte, dressed in sedum, sempervium, orostachys, lysimachia, dianthus, and *Euonymus fortunei* 'Kewensis'. She does break my rule eschewing novelty shapes—but in an unconventional way that is well worth the infraction.

appreciate new soil every couple of years, so growing it alone makes sense, since the operation of repotting is easier to carry out. Then there is the aesthetic factor. Maybe there are steps you want to punctuate with small bowls or cylinders. Or you like the look of a clutch of trough shapes placed together, an individual plant in each.

Instead of planting things together in one container, you plant the elements in separate troughs, then arrange them to be pleasing. This is a surprisingly satisfying way to trough garden. It is also a stunning way to display a collection. As things grow and change, the arrangement can be adjusted: a seasonal star can be moved to the front, a tired performer tucked away. Part of the beauty of monoculture is seeing plants happily fulfilling their destined shape and habit without undo elbowing, crowding, or overhanging from a burly neighbor. And matching a plant shape to a trough shape is a joyful meditation with almost instant results.

ASSORTED WISDOMS

As it sounds, this chapter is a miscellaneous flock of useful trough topics that will probably crop up in your trough-gardening life. They are answers to questions I often get during talks and demonstrations, and are lessons I have learned the hard way, over a couple decades of working with troughs and their miniature inhabitants.

ADDING PLANTING HOLES IN TROUGHS

An extra planting hole or two in the wall of a trough is a dramatic feature, and it offers plants a vertical position many of them crave. Though everyone who sees an example with a flourishing plant trailing lushly down the side wants to do this, it is not the easiest trick to pull off. Well, let me amend that. The longevity of the plant inserted cannot be assumed. It is best to select a sturdy performer for this role, and sturdiness will be based somewhat on where you live and what grows well for you.

This is also a hard spot physically to plant up. The best way is to plant the hole as you are filling the trough with soil.

1. FILL THE TROUGH UP TO THE LEVEL OF THE BOTTOM OF THE HOLE. Firm it in. Add more soil if you need to bring it back to the same level. This is an instance when heavier firming is good, as it helps form a platform for the roots to spread out over. The plant must be young, small, and vigorous, both by nature and because it

A big tower trough, planted with iris, succulents, and phlox on top. On the left side, *Gypsophila franzii* 'Nana Compacta'; at bottom right, *Euonymus* 'Kewensis'. Other holes contain sempervivums.

Wrap the foliage.

Roll up gently.

Insert the tube and push foliage through from the inside.

is currently growing strongly. This is not the place to put an invalid or a touchy species, or to plant late in the season. Look at the plant and at the size of the hole and decide if, a) the roots can be fitted in from the outside easily or, b) the top of the plant is smaller and can be gently pushed through from the inside out. In practice, surprisingly, the latter is usually better. A handy trick is to take a piece of slightly stiff paper and make a tube around the portion (roots or top) to be inserted.

2. GENTLY TIGHTEN THE TUBE BY TWIRLING IT INWARD until it fits the hole and slip it through. Remove the paper. Adjust the crown so it is just slightly inside the outer surface of the trough. The crown can be secured with a few shims or wedge-shaped pieces of stone.

4. BACKFILL THE REST OF THE TROUGH AND PLANT THE TOP AS USUAL. Planted side walls in troughs is a captivating feature, but it can prove to be a headache. It simply looks terrible if the hole becomes vacant. And if the top is thriving, it is difficult to replant the side without disrupting the entire top of the trough. My best solution in this case is to insert one or several cuttings of a succulent, something that roots well. If you crave a cascader, opt for one of the sedums that will oblige—*Sedum* 'Borchii Sport' and *Sedum album*

Release foliage from paper.

Instant drooler.

'Coral Carpet' are two good options. Or, sometimes, the simple rosette of a sempervivum will save the day.

FERTILIZING PLANTED TROUGHS

Freshly planted troughs will have new soil in them, soil that was (or should have been) amended at the outset. A good rule of thumb is to keep fertilizer for alpines at one eighth to one quarter strength of any recommended dosage. These plants in general come from areas of scant or impoverished soils. Too much nitrogen causes overly vigorous, leafy growth that sends the plant out of character, and may invite disease into the soft tissues. The fertilizer itself can be any number of products; avoid the harsher, processed-chemical kind. Timed-release formulas are good, as are organic choices like fish or seaweed emulsion. Avoid actual fresh manures or compost because, frankly, these are alien to the habitats of most alpines. Plus, a manure might introduce pathogens not found in alpine habitats, pathogens these little plants have not developed a defense against.

Assuming the initial plant-up included amended soil, the trough can ride on that for at least a year or two, sometimes even three. But realize that you are the only source of nutrition the plants have, so make note when anything appears to slow down, weaken, bloom less, look chlorotic, or otherwise seem unwell. Gauging by how things are doing, once it is time to fertilize, decide whether you wish to use solid or liquid. The liquids will need repeating a couple of times per season. The time-release solid fertilizer can go on once. I like to scatter more grit over the surface to cover up any fertilizer pellets, just for the sake of appearance. Be careful to not let any fertilizer of either form remain on the alpine foliage, as it can cause burning. So lightly rinse off any liquid feed and be careful to keep granular pieces off vulnerable cushions. Make your last fertilizing pass by the fourth of July. Yes, I know this is an arbitrary date, a week either side will not do any harm, but it is an easy date to remember. The reason for the deadline is to allow the plants to stop putting on new growth so they can begin the process of hardening off for the rest of the season and the winter to come.

WEEDS IN TROUGHS

Weeding is a given, even with trough gardens. But in what other garden does this job take only minutes? In my experience, there are only two circumstances in which weeds in a trough become pernicious.

The first is the appearance of the evil entity known as liverwort. This pest has dreams of empire; it can be sneaky and suddenly become entrenched. I have an absolute no-tolerance rule against this menace. I have seen it tragically disfigure beautiful cushions and plaster itself against small stems and succulent pads. It is every inch the parasite. In the interest of knowing the enemy, the botanical name for this plant is *Marchantia polymorpha*. The fruiting bodies that look like little umbrellas are called gemmae cups; it is from these that the spores disperse. The little leathery pads are called thallii. Never let the gemmae cups go into mass production. And, by the way, never use a leaf blower where liverworts grow unless you want a lot more of them. Everywhere. I will never purchase a plant whose pot contains the stuff and no, just scooping it off the soil surface does not eradicate it. I have had it jump from a trough to the cracks in a terrace and from there beyond, into the main rock garden. Once you have it, you must be ever vigilant. I have lost every plant in a choice collection in a trough while fighting these malignant pads—collateral damage, unfortunately. My arsenal at the time included Q-tips and bleach, and finally even a blow torch. It takes a lot of flame a long time to make a liverwort start to bubble.

I happen to be in a hopeful phase lately, my favored remedy being full-strength vinegar. I decant this into something with a really small spout and am exceedingly

Purchase a trailer such as this *Saponaria pumila* as a baby and plant it in a trough's side wall hole before it flowers.

careful as I pour it onto the offending pads. Vinegar will burn any foliage it splashes on, so be forewarned. You must soak the liverworts to be rid of them, and even then, a few spores may survive to reappear. Vigilance is the most important weapon one has. Don't, for even a minute, suppose that those smug leathery pads at the base of some steps on the other side of the house will do no harm. Check even the walls of the trough. Be thorough, and be ruthless.

The other cantankerous weed problem only exists if you are using genuine tufa rock in the trough. Weeds that seed into this marvelously porous material are at least as delighted to find themselves there as alpines are, and will send their roots foraging far and wide—much quicker than your chosen plants will grow. Weeds are next to impossible to pull out of tufa. Very, very young babies of unwanted guests such as oxalis and sidewalk euphorbia can be slowly, carefully pulled out with a little success. Once they are just a bit older, you will find they continually break off at the crown. Herbicides and the aforementioned vinegar will slay the weeds if you soak the tufa with it, but these "remedies" will also slay every other plant growing in or near it. If you have a prize plant growing nearby, you must decide to either wage war by hand, hoping that persistence will make the weed(s) give up eventually, or sacrifice your prize plant.

In all cases, keeping on top of potential weeds is critical. Save later trouble by placing troughs, within reason, away from weedy areas to begin with. Plan to check for weeds. This will only take minutes, a few times a year. Blithely walk past a weed with a seed head on it now, and without a doubt, you will rue it later.

WINTERING OVER

As time goes by, I employ far fewer heroic measures to winter over plants in troughs. Partly it is because I have discovered just what does well in my particular spot on the planet. I also stopped trying certain rarities, knowing my bad track record with them. Thriving plants make me happy; I am miserable watching plants barely cling to life and slowly, painfully give up the ghost. I have a "try it three times" approach, placing the plant each time in somewhat different conditions. Interestingly, after dropping a species, I have occasionally gone back many years later just to give it another try and see if anything has changed. Sometimes something has, leading to success.

If you are new to this practice of growing in troughs or are new to your garden, expect a certain amount of trial and error. A lot depends on the difficulty level of the plants you choose, and on your climate. But in my experience, a big majority of alpines do just fine if left alone over the winter. There happen to be a couple admonitions however.

Alpines are *not* houseplants. You cannot bring them into your living room for the winter and expect them to live. You would never do that to a dogwood or a peony; why a trough filled with mountain plants? You and your pets may feel cozy next to a winter fire, the trough inhabitants will not. They need vernalization, a fancy way to say they need to have their winter dormancy.

Don't leave your trough substantially elevated over the winter. A few inches is fine, but up on a deck where freezing air circulates underneath will cause repeated freezing and thawing—the exact opposite of what they want, which is to stay frozen until spring wakes them up. Leaving a trough on a retaining wall is okay, the soil below helps mitigate rapid temperature changes and frost flows downhill as a rule. Full southern or southwestern winter sun can cause winter burn. Extremely sunny winter sites are rarely successful, long term. Consider moving your troughs to a winter spot that will be less bright.

The plants inhabiting your trough are a huge part of the overwintering equation. If you live where winter slush is commonplace, dryland plants will be a challenge. Rarities from Turkey, the American West, and similar climates may need winter protection of some kind. Anything bearing silver or felted or silky foliage usually falls into this category, too; they can rot with winter wetness. Fluffy snow is a boon to alpines, keeping them insulated and in suspended animation, but sleet and slush are a curse. Some alpine growers invent wonderful roof structures. I tend to take the lazy way out and simply place a portable patio table over the trough(s). Never wrap them in plastic. Any leaves touching this will perish, and condensation and overheating can happen during any sudden warm-up, even just a bright winter day. The best protection allows for air movement, so leave adequate headroom.

If a cold frame is available and the troughs are small enough, they will be happy tucked in there for the winter. By the way, it is almost never a good idea to water alpines during the winter, when they are spending the time outside. (An alpine house is a different story.) I say "almost" because the climate can always throw us a curveball and there is only you, the gardener, to step up to the plate. Never water anything that is frozen or under snow.

One measure often taken is to cover planted troughs with evergreen branches for the winter. Don't use deciduous material—worse than useless, it will drop leaves on vulnerable cushions and mats, becoming soggy and damaging the plants. Stick with freshly cut, springy evergreens. These don't sit directly on the plants and will allow air flow underneath. Put them in place right after the soil has frozen pretty solid. And plan to remove the branches promptly at the onset of a thaw in late winter or spring. Early removal guards against new growth emerging under the shade of branches, causing tender, etiolated stems that will not survive once uncovered and exposed to a bright early-season sun. In very cold zones or on exposed high-rise terraces, people sometimes place a trough directly into an appropriately fitting Styrofoam cooler, then top that up with branches. Punching drainage holes into the cooler is a must.

Many, including myself, have been known to shovel heaps of powdery snow on top of alpine plants, either in the garden or in troughs. Besides keeping them in stasis, the snow will release, infinitely slowly, a judicious amount of moisture to the plants.

There are two very simple steps to take to protect your trough gardens at the verge of winter:

1. CHECK ALL DRAINAGE HOLES BEFORE FROST CLOSES IN. Make sure they are open and unobstructed. If a trough doesn't drain, all other precautions are pointless. Instead of frozen soil containing air, the trough will be filled with a solid block of ice. I hardly need say this, but roots cannot draw moisture in this state and plants will not remain alive long in an ice cube.

2. TOP OFF THE GRAVEL MULCH. Grit and gravel tend to disperse water, so even when the weather dumps slush or cold rain, the wetness has less chance of doing damage around the crowns of the plants.

After all this talk of survival strategies, it may sound surprising, but in most cases, it can be best to simply leave the trough alone. It is, after all, the only way to test limits: yours, the plants', the site's, and the climate's. We learn from this. It is not that heroic measures are only for the new trough gardener or the especially protective one. It is simply a fact of gardening and life that as time goes on, we all learn the vagaries of our climate better, our microclimates in particular. We may try difficult plants a few times and let some go, concentrating more on species that are better suited to our conditions. We also become better at admitting what a given plant actually needs, then either providing it or deciding to take a pass. In the end, our troughs should reflect a record of our successes. It entails a sort of Darwinian weeding out of the wimps, but it is also a testament to our tenacity and, hopefully, our increased experience.

THE ZONE CONUNDRUM

Plant hardiness zones are a man-made thing. Actually, they are a made-in-America thing; most countries don't have them. Plants aren't manufactured and stamped on the bottom with a zone number like an expiration date on a carton of milk. It strikes me that many people look at zones as a kind of guarantee, which they aren't. Zones provide a best guess at how much cold the plant can take without perishing.

An ingenious cold frame with two levels, the lower one for dormant plants.

They don't tell us how long a plant can take that lowest cold temperature. Many species can handle a brief overnight cold snap, but are damaged by prolonged deep freezes. The longer the duration of cold, the deeper the frost penetrates. Plants with far ranging or deep taproots may escape some of this frost at the deepest levels. But in a trough or any other container, plants are more vulnerable because their block of soil may freeze solid all the way through. Once an alpine, or any other plant for that matter, is put into a container above the ground, you must expect to lose what amounts to a full zone. If the trough is raised on a surface, more zonage is likely lost. Of course, there are exceptions, in the way of protected corners, blessed little microclimates, things like that.

Do not pin your hopes on providing the sunniest winter spot for troughs. As mentioned, it can cause winter burn, thawing and refreezing, the splitting of stems and trunks. Buds swell before the time is right and get blasted. All of this equals damage and it may not become evident until March or even later. Incidentally, the fact that damage often waits to become obvious to the eye is why I always err on the side of caution and don't go mucking about in my troughs early in the season, poking at shoots, testing things, tugging, or digging. In fact, poking, testing, and tugging are bad ideas at any time. The point is, give the alpines a chance to show you they are coming back before performing any operations.

Zones do not take into account how wet or dry the climate is, or how much moisture or drought the plant can take. There are plants perfectly hardy in Denver (zones 5 and 6) that routinely perish in coastal Connecticut's slightly warmer zone 6b. Why? Denver is dry.

Zones do not give us any information on how much heat a plant is comfortable with. For instance, consider plants listed as hardy from zones 5 to 9. Does that really mean they will thrive from Boston to Jacksonville, Florida? Not all places deemed zone 9 are created equal; humidity and dew point play very important parts, too. Hmm, a zone map of humidity—now *that* would be a useful tool.

That said, there are links to the hardiness zone maps for the United States and Canada at the back of this book. Use zones as a handy minimum temperature guideline that will be a little flexible, sometimes in your favor, sometimes not. When selecting your bread and butter plants, choose those that will thrive in one zone colder than yours. For the free spirit and the risk taker in you, choose a few wild cards and have fun. Plants frequently have surprises in store. A long shot may be back next year, sometimes even for several.

THE LONGEVITY (OR NOT) OF ALPINES

It's good to consider the expectations of permanency regarding alpine plants. The term "perennial" is actually a pretty variable and fluid concept. From long lived to short lived (think peony versus delphinium) to monocarpic, there is a lot of latitude. The simplest definition of perennial means plants that come back every year. But most alpines never actually left. Most are not herbaceous, especially the cushions and the mats. They only grow by increasing from last year's growth, an economy that serves them well at altitude. But that more or less permanent cushion has real drawbacks closer to sea level, or anywhere else that gets sticky and hot for protracted spans. (For alpines, a protracted span can be less than a week.) After years of growing these plants and watching their reactions, I've come to the conclusion that they can take prolonged wet, while it is cool, and heat, while it is dry. But heat and wetness together often spell disaster. Cushions filled inside with past seasons' growth will act like sponges and absorb a lethal amount of moisture.

Another thing that can cut short the life of an alpine is the plethora of pests common in most garden settings. Above timberline, you generally will not find slugs or snails, many insects, or the fungi and bacteria that can get vectored into plant tissue.

Some alpines quite literally seem to flower themselves to death. There are plants (calylophus is one example, ruellia, another) that almost behave as annuals do, they continue to flower without letting up throughout the season, and then just don't seem to have the energy left to survive the winter. It may be an internal clock problem; one of not knowing when to begin building reserves for winter or when to stop the growth of flowers and huddle down for hard times on the horizon. This clock problem plagues us with many of the plants from the antipodes. Raoulias and hebes from Australia are a prime example. They seem to like to root in midautumn, and then what? It's hard to keep babies alive through a rough winter. But even given cosseting in a frost-free greenhouse, they seem to want to slow down and rest, not surge ahead in spring.

Then there are the often-lovely monocarpic plants. These species grow only vegetatively for all kinds of various time spans, but once they get to a certain point (and only they know when that point is), a flower stalk inevitably forms and spells (with its blooming) the death of the plant. Some breathtaking plants are monocarpic; one glance at the flowers on *Saxifraga longifolia* and it is hard not to covet one. But it can break your heart, especially if you have really only wanted the superb, strappy, silver encrusted rosettes of *S. longifolia* all along, because when the flower is finished, so are those beautiful rosettes.

In the final wash, what you chose for your trough will depend on your sense of adventure and your risk tolerance. Are the temporarily present worth growing? Absolutely! *Gentiana verna* is not permanent, but who wants to go without ever growing it?

Finally, as a trough aficionado, what can you do to increase your chances of success? Practice good horticulture. Pay attention to providing the required conditions: sun, shade, drainage. Be a good plant parent. Be observant. Bite the bullet and finally find or build truly deep troughs. Consider using chunks of genuine tufa in the root zones of the plants. Add gravel and pumice to the soil mix. What is the single best step you can take to increase survival? By way of answer, here's a tiny anecdote. One April, I planted up a trough creating an outcrop of tufa rock, sandwiching choice tiny silver saxifrages between the pieces. I put it on a bench. About five weeks later, around the beginning of June, I did another. They had the same soil, aspect, ingredients, and even the same sources. They were placed on the same bench. It rained later that week. I watched for a few days as the newly planted one browned up, rotted, disappeared. The other one was perfectly fine. Years later it is still fine. The single best step you can take is to plant early in the season while it is still cool and the plants are in young spring growth. There really is no substitute.

THE LIFE SPAN OF A TROUGH

I am frequently asked how long a trough will last out in the weather. There is no one answer. There are just so many variables. How it was built and where it lives are probably the most significant of these.

In general, conditions that can shorten or lengthen the life span of the hypertufa trough will have the same effect on the plants you put in them. Some of the forces that affect trough life spans can be controlled, some can't. It is unlikely a family will move to a location a couple of zones warmer, on account of their troughs. Amazing as it may seem, things like jobs and schools seem to come first. So, there is the climate you happen to have.

There are also a few things to avoid if you want to keep the container sound. The following cautions bear repeating: don't leave a trough elevated on a deck or table for the winter. Don't place it where it will bear the full brunt of winter sun. Make sure drainage holes are not occluded at the onset of winter. In the case of empty troughs, store them in a dry place such as a garage or potting shed, or turn them upside down outside so they can't fill up with precipitation that will then freeze and expand.

Here's an easy one. Don't move your troughs around too much. That's when they break. And when you do move them, be gentle. This is sometimes easier said than done when you are trying to heft a big container and jockey it into position elsewhere. Always opt for using a cart or wagon, or even better, know when to call in support. Clear your path of obstacles beforehand, and the final placement area of anything the trough may knock against. Try to move them empty. It is astonishing how often even a well-seasoned gardener will make things harder than they need to be.

Most troughs, left in situ, will remain unscathed for eight to ten years, at least. I know many that have surpassed twenty with no trouble. However, a trough may crack the first year it is used. When this happens, the trouble is commonly tied to how it was constructed. If the hypertufa mix was not wetted sufficiently for the chemical process to kick in, then the trough will be weak, and may crack easily. Those new to building troughs often err on the side of adding less water to their mix, because it is hard to then rebalance the mix with dry ingredients if it gets too soupy. But going too far in the dry direction will keep the trough from setting up properly. A mix that includes too much peat moss can have a very similar effect; the hypertufa will be crumbly, even once dried. A final problem, and one that is harder to diagnose, has to do with low temperatures: it happens when the trough is subjected to freezing or near-freezing temperatures shortly after being made, or if the trough is built when the temperature is too cold. The necessary chemical process is inhibited under these conditions. Cement (as you are warned on the bags), is only viable when mixed within a certain temperature window. It should never be below forty degrees, and there is some evidence that even a temperature of fifty degrees for prolonged periods can impede the process. Cement must heat up during its setting up stage. If you go to unmold your trough the next morning and it feels ice cold to the touch, something is wrong.

On rare occasions, I believe, the cement itself has been the culprit in trough problems I've had; perhaps I used an old batch. I try to remember pieces I make out of material that seems problematic at the time of creation, and to note later whether more cracking occurs. It is true that cracks ruin the integrity of a piece. But a trough can live a productive and happy, long life with a non-catastrophic crack, if the trough is set in place and treated gently. I don't usually try to repair the damage. Rather than a patched-up-looking splodge of Quikcrete standing out like a sore thumb across the garden, give me the look of an honest crack any day.

TROUBLESHOOTING

Every garden created by the hand of man will, sooner or later, need that hand again to renovate it. Troughs are no exception. You walk out one day to admire your handiwork and realize all at once that you don't admire your trough creation so much anymore. What has happened? A plant or two has gone missing. That ground cover on one side is moving too aggressively, threatening that cushion. The size of the conifer is troubling you. Or it has winter scorch. Or both.

Plenty of things outgrow their space in the open garden, and this law applies inside troughs, too. Sometimes, all that's needed is a spring touch up: replace a plant, prune a little, feed and top up the mulch. Other times, well, the look of the entire planting no longer makes you happy. It may be that after an epic winter, most denizens of the trough are dead and what's left seems not worth keeping. It is always worthwhile to do an autopsy on deceased plants. By that I mean get out a small trowel and gently dig it out. Go gently so you unearth the roots. Are the roots black? Can you smell rot? Perhaps there are insects burrowed into the medium. Notice if the soil seems unduly wet, which could signal a blocked drainage hole. Or the soil may have collapsed, as mentioned in the section on soil. Peat and even perlite break down after a period of time. Or perhaps you notice that the planting medium is composed of several different soil textures in distinct clumps—a perfect lead-in to our next topic.

Bread pudding soil

This is not a good thing, and plants do not find it delicious. The growing medium inside a trough should be consistent throughout. Otherwise, strange horizons and water pathways form; there will be areas where water drains out fast and areas where the medium sops it up like a sponge. This is not good for any containerized plants, least of all finicky alpines.

There is only one way that a soil like this comes about. The gardener put it there. I once had the task of exhuming the inhabitants of a trough for someone. Every single item had died over the winter, and as I troweled them out, it became clear that each of them had a distinctly different soil. Some came out in soggy blocks; some scoops fell apart. One area was loaded with pine bark mulch and another was pretty sandy. It was patently obvious what had happened and, when I asked the trough owner, she admitted the truth. She had left all the soil from the pots the plants came in around their respective roots, and only patched them together with the soil mixture I had recommended. It resembled nothing so much as a bread pudding of soil textures. Do yourself and your alpines a favor and perform the extra step to tease out the bulk of the extant soil the plants come in. The only exception to this is when the plants have all been grown in a single type of mix, and they will be installed in the trough in the same mix. The goal is to give them all a seamless, lightly nourishing, consistent medium, so they can spread their toes into it and thrive.

Thugs

What if a plant survives too well? This is not usually an alpine problem. But it comes to pass sometimes that a plant takes dominance over a trough. There are plants that are thugs and then there are plants that are *really* thugs. This is my gentle way of warning you not to put *Sedum acre* in a trough. Of course, there really are no alpines as thuggish as a kudzu vine. Those who use troughs only to house rarities will not see this behavior, because most rarities aren't that aggressive. That's why they are rare. But sedums, thymes, antennarias, even a healthy *Androsace sarmentosa* can overreach their boundaries and encroach on neighbors. What I propose is not to ban all these potential plants from all troughs, though. Why not, in certain situations, use this tendency to advantage? Match thug for thug. Let two thugs of equal fervor duke it out among themselves. The aforementioned *Androsace sarmentosa* is fairly matched with *Campanula chamissonis*. We let succulents do this all the time. Just look at a mad attractive planting of sempervivums jostling and elbowing each other, mounding up and inching over the edges. We like this exuberant expression of vitality. And, it seems, thugs do, too. It is only a slight shift of mindset that can make of thugs a success.

The partial renovation

 Maybe just a few tenants have bitten the dust, no matter the cause. All other things being equal, if you still like the rest of the planting and design, and the other plants are in good health, it may be time for a partial renovation. The best tool for this is an old kitchen spoon, and maybe a dandelion weeder for leverage. The first order of business is to remove the dead plants, a task made easier if you first lift out any stone perched on top of their roots. Proceed to dig out as much of the old soil as you can (or dare) from the rest of the trough. Leave the roots of all other plants as unmolested as possible. You are replenishing the growing medium, and the more old soil taken out, the more fresh soil can be put in. It is up to you whether you just want to replace the plants you lost or to try a few new things. Be mindful about cultural requirements, as you were in the initial plant-up, but free yourself to experiment, too.

When it's time to completely refurbish the trough

Okay, so maybe it isn't just a few alpines that gave up the ghost over the winter. Only you as the caretaker of this miniature garden can decide when a complete do-over is warranted. Besides the look of the plants, there are a couple other things to evaluate. Perhaps all those handsome stones so carefully chosen and placed are half buried under soil and mulch, sunken almost out of sight. The soil may no longer be light and fluffy, and neither is your attitude toward your trough. Troughs ought to be adding joy to your gardening life, not sinking you into the doldrums every time you walk by. Instead of a partial fix, it may actually be easier to replant the whole thing.

If there is a remaining plant or two worth keeping, lift them out carefully, and set them in the shade. If they are not to go back into the trough, pot them up. If there are succulents you want to retain, but the patch has gotten scrappy, take some cuttings to insert later.

If the anchor plant was a shrub and it has hogged all the root room, it is going to be a little harder to remove. Before tackling this part of the operation, decide where the shrub will go once it is out. If it is slated for the garden, prepare the hole before-hand. If not, have a container ready. A big kitchen knife comes in handy here. Run it around the inside edge of the trough. You will find that roots are clinging to or even penetrating into the trough wall. Loosen and free these or simply cut through them. Then turn the trough on its side. Find a blunt handle that will fit into the drainage hole(s). In a pinch, the eraser end of a thick pencil can work, but a sturdy length of rebar is even better. Put pressure into the holes trying to free the mass of soil and roots inside. Go back with the knife to check that the sides really are loose. Try not to tug on or twist the trunk itself too much. This process can be something of a wrestling match if the shrub is deeply ensconced and stubborn. Use a dandelion weeder or hand fork to try prying the roots free from the top side. If only frustration results, it may be time to resort to a jet of water from the hose. This is a maneuver I use last because it removes a lot of soil, is messy, and leaves the roots vulnerable unless they are planted quickly (planting quickly should be the goal no matter what method of extraction is used). But I do find that wet roots are much harder to spread out and settle into the ground or a container evenly.

When the trough is empty, it is up to you whether to wash it or not. Jetting it clean with a hose is fine. Just be aware that this can dislodge hard-won and long-nurtured mosses. I usually remove all the soil from inside and replace the screen patches covering the drainage holes. I like to wash down any rocks that came out of the trough, too. It is a good idea to let things dry off before beginning the new plant-up, although it's not strictly necessary.

Always opt for fresh potting medium.

Start a replanting with washed rocks.
These were collected in Utah.

Now you can do as you please: piece back together a new incarnation with fresh plants, or treat this as a brand-new canvas. Usually, for me, the new plant-up becomes something of a hybrid of the two.

THE MIFFY LIST

All seasoned gardeners know certain plants are difficult, and there are plenty of alpines that fit the description. As you become more deeply involved with these tiny plants, and begin to cast your net farther for interesting subjects to include in your troughs, it is inevitable that you will come across a stratum of them that are often referred to as miffy. They are the Holy Grail of alpine plants. These species are: the ungettable, the ungerminatable, the ungrowable, or the unflowerable. Sometimes a single one of them combines several of these challenging features. Why consider

The difficult *Dionysia* 'Bernd Wetzel'.

these at all? Because they are ravishing. And you are bound to run across them. Not usually in the flesh, but via rumor, or at the end of the reverent finger of some enraptured collector pointing at a photo taken at twelve thousand feet. It is inevitable that you will see and probably swoon over something before you have gotten very deep into this discipline.

If you are up for a real challenge, by all means test your skill. But be aware that you may or may not have a home turf advantage. If the plant you are trying is a desert inhabitant and you live in Santa Fe, you may be in luck. But if what you crave is *Cornus canadensis*, then folks in New England and the Pacific Northwest may have luck on their side. However, home turf for some of these plants means the Himalaya, the Dolomites, the desert, Arctic tundra, or the coast of Iceland, and to gain that advantage would require moving to a pretty remote place.

Lists of the miffy—but classic—cushion plants vary. Debates have raged about what has the right to be included. Some experts would offer a list that is lofty and very short indeed. There are the impossible aretian androsaces, the glorious dionysias that prefer to grow upside down out of a deep rock fissure, the best of the drabas. A few dianthus plants may make the cut, a few saxifrages for sure. Some pundits will

Tempting Kabschia saxifrages.

allow tightly growing rare primulas, perhaps a phlox or two of the choicest kind. They may mention the one-note genera: *Kelseya uniflora*, *Shoshonea pulvinata*, or show pictures of the Andean rosulate violas.

This is a who's who of heartbreak. And believe me, I am one of the first to sigh when images of these difficult plants come up, larger than life, on the screen at a rock garden lecture. It has been years since I scribbled down the names in hopes of acquiring them. Acquisition is a challenge, but it is the easy part. It is the growing and the keeping that can lead to despair. I know from experience that they will crush your spirit if that is all you try to grow. I do hope people continue to experiment with them, though; it is the only road that might lead to them being tamed for the average gardener, and that would be wonderful. (To be honest, when a slide of a plant new to

The choice cushion of *Androsace hirtella*.

Campanula zoysii.

me pops up on the screen, of course I am scribbling madly like all the other hopeful people in the lecture hall.)

To clarify what we are up against, Merriam-Webster defines miffy as "inclined to take offense; touchy; requiring favorable conditions for growth." I would add words like resentful, petulant, disgruntled, indignant, vexed, rankled, and full of umbrage. Perhaps some of you who have tried to grow the miffy ones recognize these traits. I know a species or two that seems to have taken an irreversible umbrage toward me. And once that happens I certainly feel resentful, petulant, disgruntled, indignant, vexed, and rankled myself.

My aim is to arm you with a little foreknowledge of what lies ahead. This list is personal; it happens to be what I have bumped up against at one time or another. Many if not most of these require an alpine house to grow well. So here is my list of sirens, fetching to be sure, however fleeting. Consider yourself fairly warned.

ANDROSACE The tight, congested high mountain species of this genus are often very difficult at sea level. Enchanters such as *Androsace alpina*, *A. hirtella*, and *A. imbricata* will captivate you. The allure is the perfect dome of the cushion and small, gorgeous blooms sitting right down on the foliage spangling the entire dome. Well, the bloom will be heaviest on the sunnier half, somewhat less on the other. But to my eye this only adds to their beauty.

Convolvulus boissieri.

CAMPANULA In the crowd of bellflowers, there are many that can be grown easily. The difficult divas are a short list, among which I would include *Campanula piperi*, *C. raineri*, *C. shetleri*, and *C. zoysii*. The latter has the most distinctive blossoms, which look like small, purple-blue soda bottles, pinched closed at the ends. Some of them come from moraine environments and are used to glacially cold water running through the stony soil. Small and choice, all these plants will provide a tasty amuse-bouche for your neighborhood gastropod.

CONVOLVULUS The plants I refer to here are the low-growing mats from Turkey and Greece. I know of people with naturally xeric conditions who can grow these. The reason for craving them: aluminum foil–silver leaves. *Convolvulus boissieri* is the poster child for this kind of beauty. The white flowers are, of course, in the shape of morning glories.

Eritrichium howardii 'Blue Sky'.

DICENTRA PEREGRINA If you have seen those dicentras for sale in the King of Hearts series, this is the blood parent that gives those plants their trendsetting mojo. There are several other Hearts: 'Ivory', 'Candy', and 'Burning'. A thing to know about the series is that they are not easygoing shade perennials. They do so much better under rock garden conditions, and *Dicentra peregrina* can be thanked for that. But back to the parent. It hails from Japan, has intricate, lacy basal leaves and hearts outsized for the plant, and it demands moisture, acid soil, and cool growing conditions.

DIONYSIA Here we have buns of the highest order and the highest difficulty. Across the board, they will do better under glass, tending to rot and fall apart at the least humidity. Three considered less difficult are *Dionysia aretioides*, *D. involucrata*, and *D. tapetodes*. The "less" is relative. The exquisite allure of these domes is off the hook. Expect to sigh.

ERITRICHIUM NANUM Reginald Farrer's prose waxed ever purpler as he gushed about the mountain forget-me-not. A glance at one slide of it in habitat will bowl over even the most jaded gardener. Picture the most congested bun of small leaves utterly enveloped in silky white wool, crowned by a fleet of intensely true-blue

Inside blooms of the rare *Gentiana urnula*, from Tibet.

The foliage of *Gentiana urnula* is almost as striking as its flowers.

flowers. Attempt *Eritrichium howardii* instead. It will crush your hopes maybe thirty percent less.

GENTIANA The Himalayan gentians are fall blooming and dramatic. They are neither easy to find nor easy to keep. Some of the best-known names are: *Gentiana farreri*, *G. hexaphylla*, *G. sino-ornata*, and *G. veitchiorum*. Their glorious trumpets are that arresting blue that almost seems to have a touch of green in it, making the color lean (just barely) toward turquoise. They are opulent, and the petals are often striped and patterned. One, *G. urnula* from Tibet, captured my adoration about two decades ago and has never let go. Universally considered very difficult in cultivation, and from a remote area, I have little hope of ever seeing it in the flesh. From tightly overlapping tiny leaves, a low huddle or mat produces fat, tubby, skyward-facing chalices, white with blue-flamed bases. The coloration on these beautiful bells can be variable. I heard a rumor that someone had germinated a seed or two in Scotland once.

JANKAEA HELDREICHII This one is considered difficult to cultivate even in an alpine house, in a limestone crevice, inside a deep clay pot, in a plunge frame! It has pads of leaves with silver, silky fur; the blooms are lilac and similar in shape to gloxinia—to which it is related. I don't know. A plant that needs a refrigerated house, that can't touch the ground, or get any water at all on its leaves, ever? I think I'd just rather move on to the next challenge.

LUPINUS LEDIPUS VAR. LOBBII Although there are several other species of lupine from the American West that are small and choice, this is the one I will always remember. As a newly minted propagator at the New York Botanical Garden, I was tasked with grooming and show-potting a large number of alpines for a flower show. The grooming was done with tiny bonsai tools. We had only one *Lupinus ledipus* var. *lobbii* to show (for reasons related to why it is on this list). It had a fair number of branchlets supporting buds of pea flowers about to open. For some reason I lost my focus, and as I was going in with scissors to clip out some dead material, I misjudged and clipped off at least a third of the plant. Needless to say, I was shattered. Generously consoled, I was told, "No flower show is dependent on one *Lupinus ledipus* var. *lobbii*." It has become sort of a mantra for me.

ORIGANUM AMANUM I love oreganos and I especially love this one. It is on the miffy list because I can't grow it. What it needs is a Mediterranean climate, including dry winter weather. It is smaller than most other oreganos, featuring tiny violet trumpet flowers with long tubes that protrude out of the hop-like bracts, which are stained a rich rose red. Utterly enchanting.

PHYSOPLEXUS COMOSA This used to be classified under the genus *Phyteuma*. Whatever the name, this outlandish alpine begins with shiny, ruffled leaves. From the center emerge blooms that look like medieval maces, a globe of spikes in violet graduating to palest lavender. Tap rooted (so it hates disturbance), it also requires limestone. This one has bewitched more than geeky rock gardeners, including mountaineers. Slugs will be on the march.

PARAQUILEGIA ANEMONOIDES I have managed to germinate this and to actually produce a flower. Twice. But the plants were babies and threw out the single blossom each time in September. I have never had a fine, full-grown specimen, nor seen it in person covered in splendid lavender cups, the huddled lacy foliage forming a dome or spreading picturesquely in a crack of rock. Moving a plant is problematic. Perhaps attempting to germinate it directly in a chunk of tufa could work.

SAXIFRAGA, KABSCHIA These ravishing beauties with small, silvery rosettes and sumptuous flowers in a phenomenal range of colors are, unfortunately the flagship of miffy plants.

The ultra-miffy *Jankaea heldreichii*.

Alpine favorite *Physoplexus comosa*.

More currently, they are referred to as the *Porophyllum* saxifrages. They don't want to dry out, but they don't like soggy soil. They need plenty of light, but they must not scorch. They like it cool, but never a deep freeze with no snow cover. To date, I have not found a single variety or cultivar of the Kabschias that will live for more than a year or two in zone 6; usually they don't make it through the first summer. I think the soil just warms up too much for their liking. Even in a three-foot-deep sand plunge frame, in long-tom terra-cotta pots with a light lathe overhead, the browning of the cushions begins. One day in August, I pulled a pot out of the plunge

Temperamental beauty
Saxifraga 'Athena'.

and cradled it in the palm of my hand while I watered it. What flowed over my hand was water almost hot enough to brew some tea. It took about four or five flushes before it cooled. The roots were basically boiling in the pot. Short of moving a few zones away, there was little I could do. Most of them died that summer. Folks living in the Pacific Northwest, or Scotland, or those with an alpine house will certainly have more success. I leave it to the reader to look up and admire the beauty of these creatures. Most of us will take a stab at them a time or two. Plantspersons much more experienced than I have tried and failed, too. Ultimately, and with no hard feelings, I have let them go. It is a thing to have tried.

TRIFOLIUM NANUM A stunning clover from the Rocky Mountains (Montana, Idaho) that forms a close, ground-hugging mat. The flowers come individually, unlike the common clover head we usually see in lawns, and are a lovely graduated pink. I have killed several of them in several different sites. I know a great rock gardener in a colder zone who can grow these. Her garden is a dry one and northwest facing, with an almost ever-present breeze. *Trifolium alpinum* is another tricky one.

Clockwise, from top left:

Saxifraga 'Lutea'.

Saxifraga 'Mother Queen'.

Saxifraga 'Burserana'.

Oddly, I have had a bit of luck with *T. barnebyi* from the Wind River Range in Wyoming. Seed is hard to come by, but well worth trying.

VIOLAS OF THE ROSULATE ANDEAN KIND. These are some of the weirdest, most wonderful plant species to ever come down the evolutionary pipeline. The typical violet flowers are all that give away the genus of these crazy plants. Imagine rosettes something along the style of hens and chicks, many in warm earth tones. Then imagine violets blooming in a ring emerging between the overlapping leaves, virtually stemless. They are spectacular. And they cannot be had for love nor money. Seed is the only way to attempt to possess them, and that is hard to come by, too. Why mention them? They are astounding, they are legend that approaches myth.

Viola skottsbergiana.

Viola atropurpurea.

Swoon worthy—and isn't a little more swooning something we all can use more of in our lives?

So why did I just take you on a loop through the impossible? Surely it was not to torture the newcomer or seasoned gardener, either. Well, maybe just a little. These species have tormented me from time to time. It builds character to look at extremely beautiful things one cannot have. It is also soothing to know a failure was not necessarily your fault, and that you are, in fact, in outstanding company. I like to think that, as growers, we continue to improve our craft. And there is the faint hope that years from now, some rock gardener will find a copy of this and it will fall open to these pages. "Hmm," he may think. "We have that in our backyard. Not that hard to grow at all." The vision of a future in which outdoor troughs are spangled, festooned, and encrusted with rarities will always be worth dreaming about.

Viola beckeriana.

GLOSSARY

ALPINE HOUSE Like a little green-house that, depending on where you live, may or may not have minimal heat (to keep the house just frost free), but definitely has air conditioning to keep plants cool in summer.

ANCHOR PLANT The featured plant in a trough, often the largest in size; frequently a dwarf tree or shrub.

BAGUETTE A long trough shape with rounded ends. Looks like the loaf it is named after.

BONDING AGENT A substance some-times added to cement, ostensibly to increase strength.

BUNNERY An affectionate term for a collection of dome or cushion-shaped plants grown together or found to-gether in the wild.

BUNS AND CUSHIONS These are plants that typically grow in the shape of a hemisphere or dome. One of the most sought-after shapes for trough culture.

BUTTER STAGE A glossy, overworked stage cement can reach by too much patting and handling.

BY VOLUME Volume is the amount of space something takes up. When measuring ingredients for a batch of hypertufa (or potting soil), use one container consistently. A five-gallon bucket is great for this, but a container of any size will work and keep the ratios correct. If the recipe has two ingredi-ents and calls for a three-to-one ratio of one ingredient, then use three buckets of that ingredient and one of the other.

CATION EXCHANGE (Pronounced "cat-eye-on" not "kay-shun.") Different soils have different cation exchanges. For the layman, this refers to the soil's ability to capture nutrients that are then available to plant roots. It amounts to loam having more "parking spaces" than sand, which is less fertile.

CHEATING THE EDGE A method of chiseling the rim of a trough only partway to make it seem that the walls are thinner than they are. Used when hypertufa has hardened too much and is difficult to work.

CHLOROTIC Decreased amounts of chlorophyll that causes yellowing of plant tissues due to nutrient deficiency or disease.

COIL POT A clay pottery piece made from a long coil or rope of clay.

COURSES The name used for the rows of handfuls of hypertufa employed to build a trough. Using courses instead of simply slapping patches together makes the trough stronger and helps avoid weak spots.

CULTIVAR Abbreviation for cultivated variety. In a plant name, it is enclosed in single quotation marks.

CUSHION PLANT (*see* buns)

DROOLERS Nickname for plants that cascade, spill, or drape over the side of a container or wall.

EARTHWORKS Used here to describe using soil and rocks to create several levels inside a trough landscape.

FELT BALANCE An ideal to strive for while creating troughs. A felt balance in a piece exists when the proportions, height, thickness of walls, and texture of finish feel elegant and right. Pieces do not have to be precisely symmetrical or uniform. In fact, given that they are handcrafted, it is preferable that they do not look machine made.

FIBER MESH A synthetic fiber (not fiberglass) chopped into short pieces that are added to cement and concrete mixtures as reinforcement. Said to reduce cracking.

FINES Extremely small particles resulting from mining or milling, usually stone of some sort.

FLIPPABLE Means the trough has reached a stage of setting up or hardening in which it will not be damaged or break when being turned over.

FLOURING Just as in flouring a cake pan for ease of removal later, this is the technique of lightly dusting the surfaces around a sand mold with very dry sand just prior to beginning to build the trough. It has the desirable effect of texturing the rim and preventing the glassy look that occurs when any form of cement is cured while pressed up against a slick surface.

GLOVE UP To put on gloves. In the world of trough making, it also means to slather on a healthy dose of emollients for your skin before donning the waterproof gloves of your choice.

GRIT Pieces of stone smaller than gravel for top-dressing troughs. Grit is also a popular topdressing for seed pots. Gritting is another term for mulching troughs.

HAIRBALLS I'm sure you already know what these look like. In a trough-making context, they are made up of matted fiber mesh and can get in the way of the design and/or finishing process.

HEROIC MEASURES Anything above and beyond the usual call of duty, intended to keep difficult plants alive and (possibly) thriving. An alpine house qualifies. So does running a super-long extension cord from the house to your alpines in order to power an oscillating fan to keep them cool. There are a seemingly unlimited number of actions that qualify—gardeners are inventive and fearless in what they will attempt!

HIGH ALPINES A term used to refer to plants found growing above timberline, often at extreme altitude. Many such plants prove challenging to grow.

HYPERTUFA If you have made it this far and don't know what this is, please phone a rock gardener.

IN CHARACTER This term usually refers to plants under cultivation that display the same lean, tight, congested habit of those seen in the wild at the top of mountains or in other harsh environments. Keeping alpines in character at sea level it is not an easy trick to pull off.

LACUSTRINE Relating to or growing in lakes and other wetlands.

LEATHER STAGE In pottery making, the point at which the clay surface resembles leather, especially the feel. The surface is somewhat dry, and the mass of clay (or hypertufa) will stand up on its own. It has also lost a lot of flexibility. In trough making, it can be the point of no return with regard to attempting to knead the material into another shape. At this stage, tearing and breaking can happen.

LOOPS Nickname for clay-carving tools whose blades are circular or oval.

LUCKY CHARM SYNDROME The proclivity of new trough makers to create cute shapes that are useless for most planting purposes. Named after the cereal.

MEATBALL TROUGHS A trough construction method using balls of hypertufa to build up courses or walls in rows, still leaving the meatball shapes visible in the end product.

MIFFY Cantankerous to grow.

MONOCARPIC Describes a plant that dies after flowering. It sets seed only once in its lifetime, but the vegetative growth can live for a number of years first. Its opposite is polycarpic, in which a plant is able to flower and set seed many times in its life span.

MULTILEVEL Any troughs built with more than one level in which to plant. (*see* pocket troughs)

MYCORRHIZA A symbiotic and beneficial relationship between plant roots and the mycelium of fungus in soils. The plant provides carbohydrates to the fungus, the fungus helps the plant with the uptake of minerals. Most important for alpine growers, the fungus protects the plant roots from detrimental fungi and nematodes.

OUT OF CHARACTER The opposite of in character. (*see* in character)

OVERLAPPING JOINS A method of building up courses (or rows) of handfuls of hypertufa whereby each handful is bonded partly on the preceding handful. The overlap is stronger than placing each handful directly above another. Visualize a brick wall, with no joint directly above another.

PATTY-CAKE METHOD Handling the mixture by the handful and pressing or patting it into shape.

PLUNGE FRAME Similar to a cold frame. This is a structure of varying sizes (and heights) that is filled with a material such as sand or Turface. Pots of tricky-to-grow alpines are sunk into this medium almost to the rims. This helps winter survival rates and reduces summer collapse from excess heat, because the medium mitigates rapid changes in temperature. The sand can be watered instead of the soil in the pots (if the pots are clay), thus avoiding too much water. The frame can have a built-on winter roof to shed cold rain, slush, and all unwanted moisture—a boon when trying to grow xeric plants.

POCKET TROUGH A trough with added pockets for planting. (*see* multilevel)

THE POUR Hypertufa mix that is wet enough to pour. This consistency is most often used to fill molds that have both outside and inside walls. The molds generally are wood and can be taken apart to facilitate removal of the troughs. The Pour can also refer to the designated day for setting up a lot of these molds and filling them.

PUMICE Volcanic in origin, this lightweight igneous rock is extremely porous. Crushed pumice, for our purposes, can be a magic bullet when growing difficult or miffy plants. It can be used as an additive to potting soils or it can constitute one of the main ingredients for a mineral soil—that is, one that does not include organics.

RADICAL A radical is the root of a plant, often refers to the first root a seedling puts down.

REFLIP Once a trough has been tipped out of its mold and textured, it then needs to be turned back over for it to be finished. That's the reflip. It is mostly used in reference to disasters—the reflip is when most troughs will break if they have not set up enough.

SCORING Another term borrowed from the world of pottery. In order to secure a strong join between, say, a trough wall and the pocket you want to build onto that wall, it is advisable to rough up the existing surface with a sharp tool. Even a hair comb works for this. It helps the add-on to grab and then bond. It also helps to use a wetter mix when adding handfuls to the drier, scored side.

SLUMPING One of the most dreaded verbs in trough making—and yet, one of the most fixable. If the hypertufa is too wet or has been overworked (or both), it will succumb to gravity and slide ever downward, frightening neophytes as the walls thicken and the bottoms flood. It will seem impossible to raise slumping walls to the desired height.

SLURRY A purposely extra-wet mix used, in this context, to form a flat and even bottom on a trough that is formed upside down on a sand mold. A slurry resembles a thin mud.

SPECIFIC EPITHET This is the second word of a plant's Latin name, the species. Very often it is either descriptive or connotes a place.

TIMBERLINE The point in the mountains, at elevation, where the last trace of trees ends. Usually, but not always, this is where alpine plants begin to grow.

TRAILERS Droolers, drapers, cascaders. These are plants that flow over the side of a container.

TROUGHING The verb encompassing the entire process of building hypertufa troughs.

TURFACE A baked clay product used as a soil additive to help increase cation exchange, which increases the uptake of nutrients.

METRIC CONVERSIONS
and HARDINESS ZONES

INCHES	CENTIMETERS
¼	0.6
⅓	0.8
½	1.25
1	2.5
2	5.0
3	7.5
4	10
5	12.5
6	15
7	18
8	20
9	23
10	25

FEET	METERS
¼	0.08
⅓	0.1
½	0.15
1	0.3
2	0.6
3	0.9
4	1.2
5	1.5
6	1.8
7	2.1
8	2.4
9	2.7
10	3.0

Temperatures

$$°C = 5/9 \times (°F - 32)$$
$$°F = (9/5 \times °C) + 32$$

Plant hardiness zones

To see temperature equivalents and to learn in which zone you garden, see the U.S. Department of Agriculture Hardiness Zone Map at planthardiness.ars.usda.gov/PHZMWeb/

For Canada, go to planthardiness.gc.ca/.

RECOMMENDED READING

Barr, Claude A. 1983. *Jewels of the Plains*. Minneapolis: University of Minnesota Press.

Beckett, Kenneth (editor), and Christopher Grey-Wilson (managing editor). 1993. *Alpine Garden Society* Encyclopaedia *of Alpines*. Vols. 1 and 2. Avon Bank, Pershore, Worcestershire, UK: AGS Publications.

Bland, Beryl. 2000. *Silver Saxifrages: A Guide to the Ligulate Saxifrages and Their Culture*. UK: AGS Publications.

Carl, Joachim, John P. Baumgardt (ed.), and Martin Kral (translator). 1990. *Miniature Gardens*. Portland, OR: Timber Press.

Charlesworth, Geoffrey. 1988. *The Opinionated Gardener: Random Offshoots from an Alpine Garden*. Boston: David R. Godine.

Charlesworth, Geoffrey. 1994. *A Gardener Obsessed: Observations, Reflections, and Advice for other Dedicated Gardeners*. Boston: David R. Godine.

Davidson, B. Leroy. 2000. *Lewisias*. Portland, OR: Timber Press.

Dryden, Kath. 1988. *Alpines in Pots*. UK. AGS Publications.

Farrer, Reginald. 1985. *The Dolomites*. London: Cadogan Books.

Farrer, Reginald. 1930. *The English Rock Garden*. Vols 1 and 2. London: T. C. & E. C. Jack, Ltd.

Fingerut, Joyce, and Rex Murfitt. 2011. *Creating and Planting Garden Troughs*. Wayne, PA: B. B. Mackey Books.

Foster, H. Lincoln. 1968. *Rock Gardening: A Guide to Growing Alpines and Other Wildflowers in the American Garden*. Portland, OR: Timber Press.

Foster, H. Lincoln, and Laura Louise Foster. 1990. *Cuttings from a Rock Garden: Plant Portraits and Other Essays*. New York: The Atlantic Monthly Press.

Kelaidis, Gwen Moore. 2008. *Hardy Succulents: Tough Plants for Every Climate*. North Adams, MA: Storey Publishing.

Klaber, Doretta. 1964. *Gentians for your Garden*. New York: M. Barrows and Company.

Köhlein, Fritz, and Jim Jermyn (ed.) 1991. *Gentians*. Portland, OR: Timber Press.

Lowe, Duncan. 1996. *Cushion Plants for the Rock Garden*. Portland, OR: Timber Press.

Lowe, Duncan. 1991. *Growing Alpines in Raised Beds, Troughs and Tufa*. London: B. T. Batsford Ltd.

Lowe, Duncan, and G.F. Smith. 1977. *Androsaces*. Lye End Link, St John's, Woking, Surrey: UK. AGS Publications.

North American Rock Garden Society, Gwen Kelaidis (ed.), and Joyce Fingerut (guest ed.) 1996. *Handbook on Troughs*. Manhattan, Kansas: North American Rock Garden Society.

Perényi, Eleanor. 1981. *Green Thoughts: A Writer in the Garden*. New York: Random House.

McGregor, Malcolm. 2008. *Saxifrages: The Definitive Guide to 2000 Species, Hybrids & Cultivars*. Portland OR: Timber Press.

Mineo, Baldassare. 1999. *Rock Garden Plants*. Portland, OR: Timber Press.

Nold, Robert. 1999. *Penstemons*. Portland, OR: Timber Press.

Schenk, George. 2006. *Gardening on Pavement, Tables, and Hard Surfaces*. Portland OR: Timber Press.

Schenk, George. 1997. *Moss Gardening: Including Lichens, Liverworts, and Other Miniatures*. Portland OR: Timber Press.

Spain, John. 1997. *Growing Winter Hardy Cacti in Cold/Wet Climate Conditions*. Watertown, CT: Elisabeth Harmon.

RESOURCES

PLANTS

ALPLAINS. PO Box 489, Kiowa, CO 80117. (303) 621-2864. www.alplains.com/. A specialty seeds-only house featuring small plains and mountain plants, painstakingly collected. Terrific choices and great germination instructions.

LAPORTE AVENUE NURSERY. A wholesale-only nursery that carries wonderful alpines, conifers, and perennials. Email klehrer@msn.com to request a wholesale list.

OLIVER NURSERIES. 1159 Bronson Road, Fairfield, CT 06824. (203) 259-5609. www.olivernurseries.com. Oliver's is known for carrying an outstanding, wide, and unusual assortment of alpine plants, succulents, dwarf conifers, and troughs, both empty and planted. Also for unique annuals, perennials, trees, and shrubs, and for hard-to-find plants. Known for customer service from a knowledgeable staff. Not a mail-order nursery.

SCHREINER'S IRIS GARDENS. 3625 Quinaby Road NE, Salem, OR 97303. (503) 393-3232. www.schreinersgardens.com/. Retail and wholesale mail order with a good list of dwarf iris.

STONECROP GARDENS. 81 Stonecrop Lane, Cold Spring, New York 10516. (845) 265-2000. www.stonecrop.org. A beautiful and inspiring garden to visit. They also sell alpine plants and host a special day every April with high-quality outside vendors.

SUNSCAPES. Mailing address: 330 Carlile Avenue, Pueblo, CO 81004. Location: 4028 Nature Center Road, Pueblo, CO 81003. (719) 546-0047. sunscapes@comcast. net. Specializing in xeric and western species, many not found elsewhere. Mail order.

WRIGHTMAN ALPINES NURSERY. 480 Brandy Cove Road, St Andrews, NB E5B 2P9, Canada. (506) 529-9093. www.wrightmanalpines.com; info@wrightman alpines.com. An exceptional nursery specializing in alpine and rock garden plants, many hard to find. Some difficult plants are sold already planted in cubes of tufa to help establish them. Experts at the tufa sandwich method.

SEED AND PLANT SOCIETIES

THE ALPINE GARDEN CLUB OF BRITISH COLUMBIA (AGCBC). www.agc-bc.ca

THE ALPINE GARDEN SOCIETY (AGS). Pershore, Worcestershire, UK www.alpinegardensociety.net

THE AMERICAN CONIFER SOCIETY. PO Box 1583, Maple Grove, MN 55311. conifersociety.org

THE AMERICAN PENSTEMON SOCIETY. http://penstemons.org

THE CACTUS AND SUCCULENT SOCIETY OF AMERICA. cssainc.org

THE ERIOGONUM SOCIETY. eriogonum.org

THE NORTH AMERICAN ROCK GARDEN SOCIETY (NARGS). PO Box 18604, Raleigh, NC 27619. www.nargs.org. A great society, offering a seed exchange every year with many rarities. Chapters hold frequent plant sales; most publish newsletters. Check out the speakers at chapters online. Chapters welcome new visitors. My home chapter is the Berkshire NARGS. I also participate in events with the Manhattan and Hudson Valley chapters. The NARGS Quarterly is a world-class publication.

THE SCOTTISH ROCK GARDEN CLUB (SRGC). www.srgc.net

Note: These organizations are a fantastic resource. They offer publications on topics not found elsewhere, meetings with renowned speakers, sometimes plant sales, and seed exchanges listing seed of plants available nowhere else. Highly recommended.

ACKNOWLEDGMENTS

My gardening life has been atypical in that I have rarely gardened alone, instead doing what I do in the company of some pretty special people, in exceptional places. The New York Botanical Garden (NYBG) was the first of these. I started this book with Jimmy Martucci and I will start my thanks there, too: thank you for all you did for me. I am grateful to Margaret Falk for inviting me back to the rock garden potting shed that winter day to make my first trough. Mike Ruggiero, mentor to all School of Horticulture students, thanks for your inimitable teachings. I thank all the instructors, gardeners, curators, and scientists, who pushed us to be the best we could be. Love and thanks to my fellow students: Sarah Christ, Howie Bowie, Helen Lord, and Sallie Gregory. From the Conservatory to the Arboretum crew to the beloved "Prop" range, thanks to all of you for everything.

Those experiences overlapped with my joining the North American Rock Garden Society (NARGS); the level of knowledge represented within its membership is breathtaking. Many have become good friends. For their support, enthusiasm, wisdom, and camaraderie, I send love and thanks to Anne Spiegel, Elisabeth Zander, Joseph Tychonievich, Jacques Mommens, John Spain, Abbie Zabar, Dean Evans, Tamsin Goggin, Joyce Fingerut, Peter George, Panayoti Kelaidis, and Phyllis Gustafson. There are so many more of you. Among those gone from our midst, I will always deeply miss and remember with love the irreplaceable Midge Riggs, Larry Thomas, John Bieber, Norman Singer, and Geoffrey Charlesworth.

I doubt that anyone with my particular background could have landed at a better spot than Oliver Nurseries, where I have worked for the last two decades. Scott Jamison has created a rare, inspiring place fostering beauty and creativity; I feel blessed to work there. I thank him and the rest of the Jamison family. Indeed, this book would never have come to be without Oliver Nurseries. Gratitude goes to John Oliver, and to Joel and his late wife Ellie Spingarn, who first began growing alpines at Oliver's.

For all their help, inspiration, sweat, laughter, and love through all these seasons, thanks to Jed and Marlyse Duguid, Andrea Busk, Melanie Fox, Paul Janisch (and his whole crew each year helping with trough finishing), Vincent Loverme, Carol Osgood, Bruce Perron, Jose Pacheco, Juan Concepcion, Christopher Ashcroft, Matt Almay, and Will Hibbs. For help in the trough-making trenches, there are so many of you and I thank you all, most recently Paivi Simpson, Willa Krahn, and Chandler Vinton. Thanks to all the knowledgeable customers with whom I have shared projects and ideas. Thank you to Mike Donnelly, the designer mentioned in the preface. Without all of you, my horticultural and creative life would not have been so rich. Thank you Kim Pentergast and Joe Lazaroff, for your friendship, mini vacations on Bell Island, fabulous food, and the best view over the water.

Thank you Kristen Schleiter for your help, most recently for recommending me to Timber Press for this project. Thanks to Timber Press and my editor Tom Fischer; a special thanks to Julie Talbot who cheerfully "went through the weeds" with me, this book is better for it. Marlyse Duguid took time from an incredibly busy Yale schedule to proof and edit parts of early versions of this manuscript. She got me on a better track early on. For encouragement and guidance in the early stages, I thank Judy Glattstein. Abbie Zabar, artist, writer, and friend, thank you for the support and advice; you believed in the book from the start. Anne Spiegel offered so much help with plant lists, and did some early proofreading for me, but most cherished of all is her unwavering friendship.

Thanks to Tovah Martin for invaluable advice. Thank you to Malcolm McGregor for his crucial help tracking down photos of rare plants. Those photos came at the eleventh hour from the very generous Deiter Zschummel (*Gentiana urnula*) and the equally generous John Watson and Anita Flores Watson (rosulate violas).

The Wrightmans, including the late Harvey Wrightman, have helped this book in innumerable ways, from my first tufa drilling workshop with him, to the use of Esther's lovely photos of hard-to-grow plants. I am delighted that she and Irene will be carrying on the work of Wrightman Alpines Nursery.

Photos were taken in the enchanting garden of Lois Baylis on the Connecticut coast. Thank you for this extraordinary opportunity and for the images that enrich these pages. Thanks Lisa Robin for all the prep work and consultation before the shoot.

To Jeff McNamara, my photographer, thanks for your talent, patience, attention to detail, and esprit de corps. Being new to making a book, I found your experience proved priceless.

For pure, undiluted, amazing friendship, Kreama Southworth, Billie Chernicoff, Judy Taylor, and Athena Coroneas—thanks and love. For spending so much time in the "rag and bone shop of the heart" and on the mat, my devotion to Vicky Cook. Namaste. To the mentor of my younger years, defining a love of language, I send my love to the poet Robert Kelly.

I thank my family one and all, including the entire Fahan clan. My parents welcomed creativity, my grandparents (I was lucky to know all four), each one of them so good with their hands and with plants, showed me the value of these skills. Though I have not seen him in many years, I will always remember my brother Gary's humor and brilliance with gratitude. I send thanks and a heart full of love to my brother Mark who has always championed what I create, never failing to celebrate the joy, humor, and inspiration embedded in my words, and who brings a scientist's eye to bear; I depend upon that clarity. And, of course, my husband Joe, helping me get through the toughest botany classes, traveling to meetings, climbing mountains, and moving rocks in the backyard—you have been my most careful, honest critic and supporter; you always have my love and thanks for every single thing along the way.

PHOTOGRAPHY CREDITS

All photos by **Jeff McNamara**, except those noted below. Jeff is one of America's top magazine and advertising photographers. He has been on assignment in almost every state and continent. A native New Yorker, Jeff now lives in Fairfield, Connecticut, in a light- and laughter-filled home in the country.

Thanks to the graciousness and generosity of **Oliver Nurseries**, most of the photographs for this book were shot on-site there. Of the troughs pictured at Oliver's, the author designed and constructed all but a few, and did the planting design and execution on all. The beautiful rustic stone stairs built by Oliver Nurseries owner Scott Jamison, assisted by José Pacheco, is the setting for photos on the cover and pages 18, 38, 62, and 86. Images shot at Oliver's appear on the cover and pages 2, 17, 18, 21, 23, 24, 26, 28, 29, 30, 32, 33, 34, 35, 36, 38, 39, 40, 41, 42, 43, 44, 45, 46, 47, 48, 50, 51, 52, 53, 54, 55, 56, 57, 60, 62, 64, 66, 68, 71, 72, 73, 74, 75, 76, 77, 79, 80, 81, 82, 86, 88, 93, 94, 99, 101, 106, 109, 110, 111, 114, 115, 117, 118, 119, 120, 124, 126, 129, 132, 136, 137, 138, 139, 140, 141, 142, 144 (*Lysimachia*), 145, 146, 149 (*Campanula chamissonis*), 151 (*Gentiana acaulis*), 154, 155, 156, 158, 159, 160, 161, 163, 164 (olive dish), 165 (meatball trough), 168, 170, 172, 173, 175, 187.

Joseph Berman provided the photo on page 59.

John and Anita Watson graciously provided photos of *Viola rosulata*, pages 198, 199.

Esther Wrightman provided the beautiful photos of some hard-to-find (and hard-to-grow) alpines that appear on pages 96, 103, 104, 105, 113, 121, 125, 134, 147, 149 (*Astragalus*), 150, 151 (*Gentiana verna*), 153, 188, 189, 190, 191, 192, 195, 196, 197.

Dieter Zschummel graciously provided photos of *Gentiana urnula*, page 193.

Locations for photography include the Busk residence, pages 164–165; the garden of Lois Baylis, pages 6, 10, 13, 15, 84 (stair photo), 85, 89, 90, 95, 131, 167, 179; and the garden of the author, pages 12, 16, 59, 84 (rock-shaped trough), 102, 144 (*Astilbe* Cobblewood Series), 166, 169.

INDEX

JEFF MCNAMARA

LORI CHIPS has been committed to the exploration of alpine plants since her student days at the New York Botanical Garden. After graduating, she took a job as the propagator for the Rock Garden and the Native Plant Garden there. She has been alpine manager at Oliver Nurseries for more than two decades, expanding the rock garden collection and pressing the boundaries in the art and science of trough making and planting. Trough gardening holds a special place in her heart.

She has taught classes at NYBG, lectured to the North American Rock Garden Society, and written many articles for NARGS as well as Oliver's over the years. A botanical illustrator, Lori has had her artwork appear on covers of the NARGS Quarterly. She is the recipient of the Carleton R. Worth Award for horticultural writing and has judged at the Philadelphia Flower Show, as well as in smaller venues.

Lori lives and gardens with her husband Joe, without whom there would be less rock in the rock garden, and who is her unflagging partner, traveling to climb mountains, explore other gardens, and meet other rock gardeners. She can be reached at lorichips@optonline.net.